我的励志美文
梅花香自苦寒来

英汉对照　词汇解析　语法讲解　励志语录

马琼琼　编著

中国纺织出版社

图书在版编目（CIP）数据

我的励志美文：梅花香自苦寒来：英文 / 马琼琼编著. -- 北京：中国纺织出版社，2019.4

ISBN 978-7-5180-5094-9

Ⅰ.①我… Ⅱ.①马… Ⅲ.①英语—语言读物 Ⅳ.① H319.4

中国版本图书馆 CIP 数据核字（2018）第 119971 号

责任编辑：武洋洋　　责任校对：王花妮　　责任印制：储志伟

中国纺织出版社出版发行
地址：北京市朝阳区百子湾东里A407号楼　邮政编码：100124
销售电话：010—67004422　传真：010—87155801
http://www.c-textilep.com
E-mail:faxing@c-textilep.com
中国纺织出版社天猫旗舰店
官方微博http://www.weibo.com/2119887771
三河市延风印装有限公司印刷　各地新华书店经销
2019年4月第1版第1次印刷
开本：880×1230　1/32　印张：6.25
字数：200千字　定价：39.80元

凡购本书，如有缺页、倒页、脱页，由本社图书营销中心调换

前言

思想结晶改变人生命运，经典美文提高生活品位。曾几何时，一个字，触动你的心弦；一句话，让你泪流满面；一篇短文，让你重拾信心，勇敢面对生活给你的考验。这就是语言的魅力。通过阅读优美的英文短文，不仅能够扩大词汇量，掌握单词的用法，了解语法，学习地道的表达，更让你的心灵如沐春风，得到爱的呵护和情感的滋养。

岁月流转，经典永存。针对英语学习爱好者的需要，编者精心选取了难易适中的英语经典美文，为你提供一场丰富多彩的文学盛宴。本书采用中英文对照的形式，便于读者理解。每篇美文后都附有单词解析、语法知识点、经典名句三大版块，让你在欣赏完一篇美文后，还能扩充词汇量、巩固语法知识、斟酌文中好句，并感悟人生。在一篇篇不同题材风格的英语美文中，你总能找到引起你心灵共鸣的一篇。

读一本新书恰似坠入爱河，是场冒险。你得全身心地投入进去。翻开书页之时，从前言直至封底你或许都知之甚少。但谁又不是呢？字里行间的只言片语不总是正确的。

有时候你会发现，人们自我推销时是一种形象，等你在深入了解后，他们就完全变样了。有时故事的叙述流于表面，朴实的语言，平淡的情节，但阅读过半后，你却发觉这本书真是出乎意料的妙不可言，而这种感受只能靠自己去感悟！

阅读之乐，腹有诗书气自华；阅读之美，活水云影共天光。阅读可以放逐百年孤独，阅读可以触摸千年月光。阅读中有眼前的收获，阅读中也有诗和远方。

让我们静下心来感受英语美文的温度，在英语美文中仔细品味似曾相识的细腻情感，感悟生命和人性的力量。

编者
2018年6月

目录

01 Adrift
　　逆境求生 ··· 001

02 Beauty Is Meaningless
　　美是难以言传的 ·· 006

03 Bend, but Don't Break
　　弯而不折 ··· 012

04 Don't Give Up
　　绝不放弃 ··· 018

05 Eagle in a Storm
　　风雨中的雄鹰 ·· 022

06 Keep the Trolls Away from Your Goals
　　笼中之蟹 ··· 027

07 Sure You Can
　　相信自己 ··· 033

08 Learn From Failure
　　从失败中学习 ·· 038

09 Summon up Courage
　　迎接挑战 ··· 044

10 Up to You
　　快乐与痛苦 ·· 050

11 You'll Get Exactly What You Expect
　　期望值 ··· 056

12 Hard Work Is Good for Health
　　努力工作有利健康 ··· 062

13 Wake up Your Life
激发生活的热情 ·················· 068

14 On Idleness
论懒惰 ·················· 073

15 Thoughts for a New Year
新年沉思 ·················· 080

16 What's Your Spiritual IQ?
什么是你的精神智商? ·················· 087

17 Life Without Failure
人生没有失败 ·················· 094

18 The Strenuous Life
勤奋的生活 ·················· 101

19 Flying Like a Kite
像风筝一样飞翔 ·················· 108

20 Attitude Is Everything
态度决定一切 ·················· 113

21 Dell's Story
戴尔的故事 ·················· 117

22 Benefits from Occasional Stress
从偶尔的压力中受益 ·················· 122

23 We Never Told Him He Couldn't Do It
我们从不说他做不到 ·················· 127

24 There Are No Such Setbacks That We Could Not Overcome
人生没有过不去的坎 ·················· 132

25 Shower Brings Flowers
骤雨带来似锦繁花 ·················· 137

26 The Road to Success
成功之路 ·················· 142

27 Sleeping Through the Storm
未雨绸缪 ·················· 148

Contents 目录

28 Seek the Seed of Triumph in Everyday Adversity
梅花香自苦寒来 ································· 153

29 The Answer Is Right There Above You
希望就在前方 ····································· 158

30 Dark Clouds Always in the Past
乌云总会过去 ····································· 163

31 Never Give Up
永不放弃 ·· 169

32 Hard Life
艰辛的人生 ·· 175

33 If I Rest, I Rust
如果我休息，我就会生锈 ······················ 181

34 Suppose Someone Gave You a Pen
假如有人送你一支笔 ···························· 186

01 Adrift
逆境求生

In 1982, Steven Callahan was crossing the Atlantic alone in his sailboat when it struck something and sank. He was floating in a **life raft**, alone. When three fishermen found him seventy-six days later (the longest anyone has survived a **shipwreck** on a life raft alone), he was still alive.

His account of how he survived is fascinating. But the thing that caught my eye was how he managed to keep himself going when all hope seemed lost, when there seemed no point in continuing the struggle, when he was suffering greatly, when his life raft was **punctured** and after more than a week struggling with his weak body to fix it, it was still leaking air. Giving up would have seemed the only sane option.

When people survive these kinds of circumstances, they do something with their minds that gives them the courage to keep going. Many people in similarly desperate circumstances give in or go mad. Something the survivors do with their thoughts helps them find the **guts** to carry on in spite of overwhelming **odds**.

"I tell myself I can handle it," wrote

1982年，史蒂文·卡拉汉乘船独自穿越大西洋的时候，帆船因撞击沉了。他依靠救生筏在海面上漂浮着。七十六天之后，当三个渔夫发现他的时候，他还活着（这是在船只失事中个人依靠救生筏最后获救的最长时间纪录）。

关于自己是如何幸存下来的，他的说法很有意思。但是最引我注意的是，当所有的希望全部破灭，当没有理由再继续坚持，当他遭受那么大的痛苦，当他拖着虚弱的身体在一周多时间里还没能修好漏气的救生筏时，他是如何坚持下来的。看上去放弃才是唯一明智的选择。

从这种环境中幸存下来的人，他们的毅力和信念鼓励他们继续坚持。在这种令人绝望的环境中，很多人都屈服了或者发疯了。但是幸存者的毅力和信念让他们满怀勇气，即使面对无法抗拒的趋势也要坚持下去。

卡拉汉在他的叙述中写道："我告诉自己我可以的。

Callahan in his **narrative**. "Compared to what others have been through, I'm fortunate. I tell myself these things over and over, building up **fortitude**..." I wrote that down after I read it. It struck me as something important. And I told myself the same thing when my own goals seemed far off or when my problems seemed too overwhelming. And every time I've said it, I have always come back to my senses.

The truth is our circumstances are only bad compared to something better. But others have been through much worse. I've read enough history to know you and I are lucky to be where we are, when we are, no matter how bad it seems to us compared to our **fantasies**. It's a sane thought and worth thinking.

So whatever you're going through, tell yourself you can handle it. Compared to what others have been through, you're fortunate. Tell this to yourself over and over, and it will help you get through the rough spots with a little more fortitude.

与那些经历灾难的人相比，我是幸运的。我一遍遍地告诉自己，以此来建立信念。"我读完这些话后就写了下来。这些话深深地震撼了我。当我的目标看起来非常遥远的时候，或者当我面临的困难难以抗拒的时候，我也曾告诉自己这些。每一次我这样说的时候，我总会重新回到理智的状态中。

确实，我们身处的环境总是跟好的比起来才显得非常糟糕。但是总是有一些人经历着更加糟糕的事情。我读过很多历史资料，明白了无论现实跟幻想比起来有多残酷，其实我们都很幸运，处在这个时代、做自己本身这个人。这个观点非常明智，也很令人深思。

所以，无论你将要经历什么困境，告诉自己你可以的。与其他人经历的那些相比，你是幸运的。不断这样告诫自己，这会帮你增添毅力，克服困境。

单词解析 Word Analysis

life raft *n.* 救生筏

例 The life raft was buoyed up by two airtight oil drums.
救生筏是用两只密封的油桶浮起来的。

Adrift 逆境求生 01

shipwreck ['ʃɪprek] *n.* 遇难船；海难；船只失事
例 The whole family perished in a shipwreck.
这一家人在一次海难中全部丧生。

puncture ['pʌŋktʃər] *v.* 刺穿；削弱
例 Our tires do not puncture easily.
我们的轮胎不易爆破。

guts [gʌts] *n.* 内脏；勇气（只用复数）
例 It takes a lot of guts to do so.
你这样做很需要勇气。

odds [ɑːdz] *n.* 概率；可能性；差别；投注赔率；让步；优势
例 His odds are very poor after he sprained his wrist.
他扭伤了手腕，获胜的可能性极小。

narrative ['nærətɪv] *n.* 故事；叙述
例 His adventure made an interesting narrative.
他的冒险是个有趣的故事。

fortitude ['fɔːrtətuːd] *n.* 刚毅；坚毅；不屈不挠
例 I know that my body lacks the fortitude and courage of a strapping young man, and that I cannot find my niche in life.
我知道我身上缺少一个男子汉所应该有的刚毅和果敢，顶不起一片天空。

fantasy ['fæntəsi] *n.* 幻想
例 He is unable to divorce fantasy from reality.
他不能将幻想与现实分开。

语法知识点 Grammar Points

① In 1982, Steven Callahan was crossing the Atlantic alone in his sailboat when it struck something and sank.

这个句子中有一结构 "sb. be doing when..."，表示 "当……的时候发生了……"。
例 I was doing my homework when Mary called me.
当我做作业的时候，玛丽打电话给我。

② **But the thing that caught my eye was how he managed to keep himself going when all hope seemed lost, when there seemed no point in continuing the struggle, when he was suffering greatly, when his life raft was punctured and after more than a week struggling with his weak body to fix it, it was still leaking air.**

这个句子比较长，让我们逐步分析。第一个that引导的是定语从句，先行词是thing，that在从句中做主语。catch one's eye 是固定搭配，表示"吸引某人注意力"，注意eye要用单数。was后面是how引导的表语从句。这里有两个固定搭配：1. manage to do sth. 设法成功做某事。2. keep sb. doing 让某人一直做某事。

例 Disguising himself as an old man, he managed to make his way through the enemy lines.
他化装成一个老头儿，设法通过了敌人的封锁线。
The police keep the traffic moving.
警察使交通畅通无阻。

后面是四个由when引导的时间状语从句。其中，第二个从句里有一个句型是"there be / seems / seemed no point in doing sth."，表示"没有理由做某事，做某事没用"。最后一句中，注意单词leak的用法。leak的基本含义是"漏"，指由于包装破损或没有妥善包装而引起内部物质的外泄，通常是指液体或气体，引申可指新闻或秘密等。leak可做及物动词，也可做不及物动词。用做及物动词时，后接名词做宾语。

③ **I've read enough history to know you and I are lucky to be where we are, when we are, no matter how bad it seems to us compared to our fantasies.**

句中no matter how就相当于however，后面引导的是让步状语从句。

例 No matter how hard he may try, he will not succeed.
不管他怎么努力去干都不会成功的。
No matter how many prototypes we make, we just cannot get it right.
不管做多少次样品，我们都无法满意。

还要注意compare的用法。句中是"compare to"，意思是"同……相比"，一般用于两个不同性质的事物比较。而compare with 的意思是"把……跟……比较"，一般用于两个同类事物之间，着重区别。

例 We may well compare the little girl to a kitten.
我们可能把这个小姑娘比作小猫来看待。
She compares me with my sister.
她把我和我妹妹进行比较。

经典名句 Famous Classics

1. Worrying does not empty tomorrow of its troubles, it empties today of its strength.
忧虑不会消除明天的麻烦，只会消除今天的力气。

2. As selfishness and complaint cloud the mind, so love with its joy clears and sharpens the vision.
自私和抱怨是心灵的阴暗，愉快的爱则使视野明朗开阔。

3. All things will come round to him who will but wait.
只要耐心肯等待，一切都会按时来。

4. Patience is bitter, but its fruit is sweet.
忍耐是痛苦的，但它的果实是甜蜜的。

5. Zeal without knowledge is fire without light.
热情而无知，犹如无光之火。

6. The man who has made up his mind to win will never say "impossible".
凡是决心取得胜利的人是从来不说"不可能的"。

7. It is not the fine coat that makes the gentleman.
使人成为君子的并不是讲究的衣着。

02 Beauty Is Meaningless
美是难以言传的

A young man sees a sunset and, unable to understand or to express the emotion that it **rouses** in him, concludes that it must be the **gateway** to a world that lies beyond. It is difficult for any of us in moments of intense **aesthetic** experience to resist the suggestion that we are catching a glimpse of a light that shines down to us from a different **realm** of existence, different and, because the experience is intensely moving, in some way higher. And though the **gleams** blind the eyes and **dazzle**, yet they do convey a **hint** of beauty and **serenity** greater than we have known or imagined. Greater too than we can describe, for language, which was invented to convey the meanings of this world, cannot readily be fitted to the uses of another.

That all great art has this power of suggesting a world beyond is undeniable. In some moods, nature shares it. There is no sky in June so blue that it does not point forward to a bluer, no sunset so beautiful that it does not wake the vision of a greater beauty, a vision which passes before it is fully

年轻人看到日落，由于无法理解或表达心中激起的那种强烈感情，便断定日落处一定是通往遥远世界的大门。我们任何人在强烈感受到美的时刻都不禁联想到：我们似乎瞥见从一个不同世界射向我们的一线光芒，不仅不同，而且因为这种美具有强烈的感染力，所以在某种程度上更高级。还有，尽管这光芒使人眼花缭乱，但它确实传达了一种我们未曾经历的和无法想象的美和静谧的启示。这种美和静谧是我们所不能描述的，因为人们创造语言的目的是表达我们的世界的各种意义，无法轻易地运用于另一个世界。

不可否认，一切伟大的艺术都具有使人超尘脱俗的浮想的力量。在某种状态下，大自然就具有这种魅力。六月的天空不是蓝得不能再蓝，日落不是美得不能再唤起一个更美的景象，一个未被饱览就消失的而且在消失的时候留给人们一种莫名的渴望和遗憾的景象。但是，如果这个世界不只是一

Beauty Is Meaningless
美是难以言传的

glimpsed, and in passing leaves an indefinable longing and regret. But, if this world is not merely a bad joke, life a **vulgar** flare **amid** the cool **radiance** of the stars, and existence an empty laugh braying across the mysteries, if these intimations of a something behind and beyond are not evil humor born of indigestion, or **whimsies** sent by the devil to mock and **madden** us, if, in a word, beauty means something, yet we must not seek to **interpret** the meaning.

If we glimpse the unutterable things, it is not wise to try to utter it, nor should we seek to invest with significance which we cannot grasp. Beauty in the terms of human meanings is meaningless.

场恶作剧的话，如果生命不只是惨淡星光里的平凡的一闪的话，如果存在不只是神秘宗教发出的一阵空虚的笑声的话，如果对某种玄妙事物的暗示不是由于消化不良而引起的不好情绪，或者不是一种魔鬼送来嘲笑我们并使我们发狂的怪念头的话，一句话，如果美有某种意义的话，我们千万不要设法去阐明它的意义。

如果我们瞥见难以言传的东西，企图用语言把它表达出来是不明智的。我们也不应该设法给我们所不理解的事物赋予意义。从人生各种意义来看，美是难以言传的。

单词解析 Word Analysis

rouse [raʊz] *v.* 唤醒；激起

例 He's very hard to rouse in the morning.
他早晨很难被唤醒。

gateway ['geɪtweɪ] *n.* 门；通路

例 We stood by the gateway watching the sunset.
我们站在门口看日落。

aesthetic [esˈθetɪk] *adj.* 美学的；审美的；有美感的

例 From an aesthetic point of view it's thetic.
从美学观点来说，这是个武断的看法。

realm [relm] *n.* 领域；王国
- 例 The material realm is one area that everyone relates to.
  物质领域是与每个人有联系的一个地方。

gleam [gliːm] *n.* 微光；闪光；闪现
- 例 I could see the faint gleam of light in the distance.
  我能看见远处微弱的灯光。

dazzle ['dæzl] *v.* 使眼花；使赞许
- 例 His eyes dazzled before the strong light.
  他面对强光头晕目眩。

hint [hɪnt] *n.* 暗示
- 例 There were subtle hints in his letter.
  他的信中有些微妙的暗示。

serenity [sə'renəti] *n.* 宁静；沉着
- 例 I enjoyed the serenity and the peacefulness when I was in the church.
  当我身处大教堂时感到平和与宁静。

vulgar ['vʌlɡər] *adj.* 通俗的；粗俗的；乡土的
- 例 Her taste in clothing is rather vulgar.
  她的穿着相当俗气。

amid [ə'mɪd] *prep.* 在其间；在其中
- 例 He sat down amid deafening applause.
  他在震耳欲聋的掌声中就座。

radiance ['reɪdiəns] *n.* 光辉；辐射
- 例 The radiance of electric lights radiates from the ceiling.
  电灯的光芒从天花板上辐射下来。

whimsy ['wɪmzi] *n.* 怪念头；异想天开；心情浮动；反复无常
- 例 Some show cars are pure whimsy, dreamed up by young designers at play.
  展出的车型中有些纯属异想天开，只是年轻设计师们闲来无事的凭空想象。

Beauty Is Meaningless 美是难以言传的

madden ['mædn] 使发狂；激怒

例 I cannot reconcile myself to this idea—it would madden me.
我不能接受这种想法，它会使我发疯的。

interpret [ɪn'tɜːrprɪt] 口译；解释；翻译；诠释

例 Not everybody agreed with the way she interpreted the violin concerts, but it was still a technically perfect performance.
并非每个人都同意她对那首小提琴协奏曲的诠释，但是她的演奏在技巧上仍是无懈可击。

语法知识点 *Grammar Points*

① **A young man sees a sunset and, unable to understand or to express the emotion that it rouses in him, concludes that it must be the gateway to a world that lies beyond.**

这是一个较为复杂的句子。句子的主干"A young man sees a sunset and concludes that it must be the gateway to a world that lies beyond."中有两个that，其中第一个that引导的是宾语从句，that 在从句中不充当成分；第二个that引导的是定语从句，先行词是world，that 在从句中充当主语。另外，两个逗号中间的部分"unable to understand or to express the emotion that it rouses in him"做主语补语，是补充解释说明主语"A young man"的。

例 He arrived at home at ten p.m., tired and hungry.
他晚上十点才到家，又累又饿。

② **It is difficult for any of us in moments of intense aesthetic experience to resist the suggestion that we are catching a glimpse of a light that shines down to us from a different realm of existence, different and, because the experience is intensely moving, in some way higher.**

这个句子用了"It is+adj.+ for sb. to do sth."这一句型。其中，it做形式主语，真正的主语是后面的to do 不定式。因为主语较长，为了避免头重脚轻，所以用了it来做形式主语。

例 It is very necessary for students to study hard.
对学生来说，用功读书是很必要的。

句中有两个that。其中，第一个that 引导的是同位语从句，suggestion是先行词，从句是对suggestion的解释说明，从句是一个完整的句子，that在从句中不充当成分；第二个that引导的是定语从句，先行词是light，that 在从句中充当主语。

例 The news that the team of our school won the game excited us.
我们学校的球队赢得比赛的消息令我们十分振奋。

后面的两个逗号之间的 "because the experience is intensely moving" 是插入语。分析句子结构时可忽略不看。

③ **If we glimpse the unutterable things, it is not wise to try to utter it, nor should we seek to invest with significance that which we cannot grasp.**

这个句子中有部分倒装结构 "nor should we seek to..."。以no, nor, only in this way, never, little, often, not only, not until, hardly, scarcely 等词引起的句子，常用倒装语序。

例 Under no circumstances must a soldier leave his post.
无论在什么情况下，士兵都不会离开他的岗位。

I couldn't answer the question. Nor could anyone else answer in our class.
我回答不出这个问题，我们班上的其他人也都回答不出来。

经典名句 Famous Classics

1. Make the best of a bad business (or job or bargain).
   身处山穷水尽，力争柳暗花明。

2. How often are we to die before we go quite off the stage? In every friend we lose a part of ourselves, and the best part.
   在我们完全离开这个世界以前，我们是怎样慢慢死去的呢？每次失去一个朋友，我们就有一部分死去了，而且是最好的那一部分。

3. True mastery of any skill takes a lifetime.
   对任何技能的掌握都需要一生的刻苦操练。

4. Sweat is the lubricant of success.
   汗水是成功的润滑剂。

5. You can make more friends in two months by becoming interested in other people than you can in two years by trying to get other people interested in you.
   通过对别人感兴趣来交朋友比试图让别人对你感兴趣来交朋友要快得多。

6. If you are doing your best, you will not have to worry about failure.
   如果你竭尽全力，你就不用担心失败。

7. Energy and persistence conquer all things.
   能量和坚持可以征服一切事情。

读书笔记

03 Bend, but Don't Break
弯而不折

One of my fondest memories as a child is going by the river and sitting **idly** on the bank. There I would enjoy the peace and quiet, watch the water rush **downstream**, and listen to the **chirps** of birds and the **rustling** of leaves in the trees. I would also watch the bamboo trees bend under pressure from the wind and watch them return **gracefully** to their upright after the wind had died down.

When I think about the bamboo tree's ability to bounce back, the word **resilience** comes to mind. When used in reference to a person, this word means the ability to readily recover from shock, depression or any other negative situation. Have you ever felt like you are about to **snap**? Have you ever felt like you are at your breaking point? Thankfully, you have survived the experience to live to talk about it. During the experience you probably felt a mix of emotions that threatened your health. You felt emotionally **drained**, mentally exhausted and you most likely **endured** unpleasant physical **symptoms**.

Life is a mixture of good times

关于童年，我最美好的回忆就是去小河旁，懒散地坐在岸边。在那里我享受着平和安静，看着水直流而下，听着鸟叫声和树叶的沙沙声。我还观察到竹子在风的压力下弯曲，然后在风停后优雅地恢复直立状态。

当我思考竹子恢复原状的能力时，脑海中浮现出了"适应力"这个词。把这个词用在人身上，意味着受到冲击、沮丧或是其他消极情况之后易恢复的能力。你曾经有没有一刻觉得你快要崩溃了？或是觉得就在崩溃的那一点上了？真是幸运，你已经有了那种经历，现在还能生龙活虎地来谈论它。在那次经历中，你可能会有一系列威胁到你身心健康的混合的情绪。你感到情感上消耗殆尽，心理上疲惫不堪，很可能身体上也忍受着痛苦。

生活中有好有坏，有快乐也有悲伤。下次你再经历那种痛苦得几乎把你推到崩溃边缘的时刻时，要学会弯而不折。尽你最大的努力让那一刻的你

Bend, but Don't Break 弯而不折

and bad times, happy moments and unhappy moments. The next time you are experiencing one of those bad times or unhappy moments that take you close to your breaking point, bend but don't break. Try your best not to let the situation get the best of you. A measure of hope will take you through the unpleasant moments. With hope for a better tomorrow, things may not be as bad as they seem to be.

保持最好的状态。满怀希望会帮助你克服那些痛苦。心里想着明天会更好，事情可能不像它们看起来那么糟糕。

单词解析 Word Analysis

idly ['aɪdli] *adv.* 懒散地；漫不经心地

例 She sat in the sun, idly sipping a cool drink.
她坐在阳光下懒洋洋地抿着冷饮。

downstream [ˌdaʊn'striːm] *adv.* 朝下游方向

例 Is the water polluted at source or further downstream?
河水是在源头还是在流出之后受到污染的？

chirps [tʃɜːps] *n.* 啾啾

例 My cricket chirps against thy mandolin.
我的蟋蟀在跟你的琵琶应和。

rustling ['rʌslɪŋ] *n.* 瑟瑟声；沙沙声

例 There was a rustling of dresses, and the standing congregation sat down.
站着的人们在一片衣服的沙沙声中坐了下来。

gracefully ['greɪsfəli] *adv.* 优美地；斯文地

例 He dived gracefully into the water.
他动作优美地跳入水中。

resilience [rɪˈzɪliəns] *n.* 适应力；弹性

例 She has shown great resilience to stress.
她对压力表现出了极大的适应能力。

snap [snæp] *v.* 噼啪作响；崩塌；砰地关上；猛咬；谩骂；拍摄

例 Most pine snaps as it burns.
大多数松木燃烧时都发出断裂声。

drain [dreɪn] *v.* 排出；排干；喝光；耗尽

例 We must dig a trench to drain away the water.
我们必须挖一条沟排水。

endure [ɪnˈdʊr] *vt.* 容忍

例 I could not endure the insolence of his behavior.
我不能再忍受他那傲慢无礼的行为了。

symptoms [ˈsɪmptəmz] *n.* 症状

例 She developed symptoms of consumption.
她显示出肺病的症状。

语法知识点 Grammar Points

① One of my fondest memories as a child is going by the river and sitting idly on the bank.

这个句子中，one of+可数名词的复数，后面的谓语动词用单数。

例 One of my classmates is from London.
我有一个同学来自伦敦。

as 在这里是"作为"的意思，用作介词。

例 As a policeman, he has the responsibility to protect us.
作为一名警察，他有责任保护我们。

As a schoolboy, he showed every sign of genius.
当他还是个小学生的时候，就显示出了天资聪慧。

Bend, but Don't Break 弯而不折 03

② I would also watch the bamboo trees bend under pressure from the wind and watch them return gracefully to their upright after the wind had died down.

这个句子中，would 表示过去常常做的事情。
watch sb./sth. do 看某人/某物做某事的全过程；watch sb./sth. doing 看某人/某物正在做某事

例 He had watched me grow from childhood.
他是看着我长大的。
We were standing there watching them skipping rope.
我们站在那里看他们跳绳。

die down 渐渐消失；平息；变弱

例 Open the air hole; the fire is dying down.
把气孔打开，火要熄了。
The fire died down, so we put more coal on it.
炉火变弱了，所以我们再加了些煤。

③ When I think about the bamboo tree's ability to bounce back, the word resilience comes to mind.

bounce back （受挫折后）恢复原状

例 I bounce back from disappointment.
我很快就能从挫折中恢复过来。
It took 6 weeks to bounce back from the jungle.
从混乱恢复原状用了六周的时间。

come to mind 想到

例 A number of possibilities come to mind.
我脑里出现了好几种可能性。
For most people, only two options come to mind.
对大多数人来说，只有两个选择浮现脑海。

④ When used in reference to a person, this word means the ability to readily recover from shock, depression or any other negative situation.

这个句子中，因为从句和主句的主语一致，所以从句中的主语被省略了。原句应该是 "When this word is used in reference to a person, it means the ability to readily recover from shock, depression or any other negative situation."

in reference to 关于；有关

例 In reference to the interview our representative had with you, we offer our service as shipping agent.
按照本公司代表与您的洽谈结果，本公司愿作为贵公司的船运代理人。
He spoke in reference to Boy Scouts.
他讲了些关于童子军的事情。

recover from 是固定搭配，表示"从……中恢复过来"。

例 He's now fully recovered from his stroke.
他现已从中风完全康复了。

经典名句 Famous Classics

1. Every noble work is at first impossible.
   每一个伟大的工程最初看起来都是不可能做到的！

2. We improve ourselves by victories over ourselves. There must be contests, and we must win.
   我们通过战胜自己来改进自我。那里一定有竞赛，我们一定要赢！

3. One friend in a lifetime is much, two are many, three are hardly possible. Friendship needs a certain parallelism of life, a community of thought, a rivalry of aim.
   一生中有一个好友已经足够，两个就算很多，三个几乎不可能。友谊需要两人之间的平等，思想上的统一，以及实现共同目标的竞争。

4. False friends are like our shadow, keeping close to us while we walk in the sunshine, but leaving us the instant we cross into the shade.
   损友如同我们的影子，在阳光灿烂时与我们形影不离，在黑暗惨淡时就不见踪影。

5. A man is not old as long as he is seeking something. A man is not old until regrets take the place of dreams.

Bend, but Don't Break
弯而不折 03

只要一个人还有追求，他就没有老。直到后悔取代了梦想，一个人才算老。

6. One's real value first lies in to what degree and what sense he set himself.
   一个人的真正价值首先取决于他在什么程度上和在什么意义上从自我解放出来。

7. Don't try so hard, the best things come when you least expect them to.
   不要着急，最好的总会在最不经意的时候出现。

读书笔记

04 Don't Give Up
绝不放弃

If we should ever accomplish anything in life, let us not forget that we must **persevere**. If we would learn our lessons in school, we must be diligent and not give up whenever we come to anything difficult. We shall find many of our lessons very hard, but let us consider that the harder they are, the better they will do to us if we will persevere and learn them **thoroughly**. But there are some among us who are ready to give up when they come to a hard example in mathematics and say, "I can't do this." They never will if they feel so. "I can't" never does anything worthwhile; but "I'll try" accomplishes **wonders**.

Let us remember that we shall meet with difficulties all through life. They are in the **pathway** of everyone. If we will only try and keep trying, we shall be sure to **conquer** and overcome every difficulty we meet with. If we have a hard lesson today, let us **strive** to learn it well and then we shall be prepared for a harder one tomorrow. And if we learn to master hard lessons in school, it will prepare us to overcome the hard things that we shall meet in life, when our school days are over.

不要忘记，在人生的道路上，要想做成什么事，我们必须持之以恒。如果我们在学校里想要学好功课，就必须得勤奋，任何时候遇到难题都不要放弃。我们会发现，许多功课非常难，但是我们得记住，那些功课越难，将来对我们的益处就越大，只要我们能持之以恒，完全弄懂。不过，我们当中有一些人，一遇到数学难题就轻易放弃，说："这道题我做不出来。"如果他们这么认为，那他们永远也做不出来。说"我不能"的人永远干不成任何有价值的事，而说"我会努力"的人则可以创造奇迹。

让我们记住，在我们一生中，总要遇到各种难题。这些难题就横亘在每一个人的人生道路上。只要我们努力，再努力，就一定会征服所遇到的每一个困难。假如我们今天功课上遇到一个难题，那就让我们竭力解决它，然后我们就可以做好准备应付明天更大的难题。假如我们在学校里学会驾驭功课上的难题，将来离开学校后，我们就可以准备好克服在人生道路上遇到的各种难题。

Don't Give Up 绝不放弃 04

单词解析 Word Analysis

persevere [,pɜːsə'vɪr] *v.* 坚持；不屈不挠

> He was hopeless at French, but his teacher persevered with him.
> 他怎么也学不会法语，可是老师仍锲而不舍地帮助他。

thoroughly ['θɜːrəli] *adv.* 彻底地；完全；非常

> We shall thoroughly smash the scheme of the enemy.
> 我们要彻底粉碎敌人的阴谋。

wonder ['wʌndər] *n.* 惊奇，惊愕；奇迹，奇观

> It's a wonder that the child came through without a scratch.
> 这孩子竟能安然无恙地脱险，真是奇迹。

pathway ['pæθweɪ] *n.* 路；径

> The pathway was rough and covered with little stones.
> 这条路高低不平，铺满了小石头。

conquer ['kɑːŋkər] *vt.* 征服；克服；战胜 *vi.* 得胜

> Conquer the desire, or they will conquer you.
> 你不战胜欲念，欲念就会征服你。

strive [straɪv] *vi.* 奋斗；努力；力求；斗争

> We should all strive to reunify the motherland.
> 我们共同努力，实现祖国统一。

语法知识点 Grammar Points

① **We shall find many of our lessons very hard, but let us consider that the harder they are, the better they will do to us if we will persevere and learn them thoroughly.**

这个句子中有一个 if 引导的条件状语从句，另外有以下几个短语词组。
find sth. +adj. 发现某物……

> I found it very difficult to adapt myself to things all around here.
> 我发现我很难使自己适应周围的事物。

let sb. do 让某人干某事

同义词组还有：have / make sb. do 以及 get sb. to do

例 I won't let him get away with that excuse.
我不会让他用那种借口蒙混过去。

the+比较级，the+比较级 越……就越……

例 The harder you study, the higher mark you will get.
你越用功读书，你得到的分数就越高。

do good to sb./sth./doing 对……有好处

例 To do good to friend and evil to enemy.
对友须善，对敌须恶。
Exercise will do good to your health.
锻炼将对你的健康有益。

② **Let us remember that we shall meet with difficulties all through life.**

这个句子是一个宾语从句，从句部分做remember的宾语。

meet with 碰见；遇到；经受；符合

例 I hope the arrangements meet with your approval.
我希望这些安排会得到你的同意。
In the prosecution of his duties he had met with a good deal of resistance.
他在执行职务中遇到许多阻力。

all through 在整个……期间；一直

例 He lived in the house all through his life.
他一生都住在那栋房子里。

③ **And if we learn to master hard lessons in school, it will prepare us to overcome the hard things that we shall meet in life, when our school days are over.**

这个句子中，前面是if引导的条件状语从句，用一般现在时，主句用一般将来时。后面有一个that引导的定语从句，先行词是the hard things，that在从句中不做任何成分。这个定语从句中还包含一个when引导的时间状语从句。

Don't Give Up 绝不放弃

经典名句 Famous Classics

1. One needs 3 things to be truly happy living in the world: something to do, someone to love, something to hope for.
   在这个世界我们只需拥有三件事便可真正快乐:有自己喜欢的事业；有所爱之人；充满希望。

2. Do not, for one repulse, give up the purpose that you resolved to effect.
   不要只因一次失败，就放弃你原来决心想达到的目的。

3. Don't part with your illusions. When they are gone you may still exist, but you have ceased to live.
   不要放弃你的幻想。当幻想没有了以后，你虽然还可以生存，但虽生犹死。

4. If you have no enemies you are apt to be in the same predicament in regard to friends.
   如果你没有敌人，那么很有可能你也没有朋友。

5. I want to bring out the secrets of nature and apply them for the happiness of man. I don't know of any better service to offer for the short time we are in the world .
   我想揭示大自然的秘密，用来造福人类。我认为，在我们的短暂一生中，最好的贡献莫过于此了。

6. Ideal is the beacon. Without ideal, there is no secure direction; without direction, there is no life.
   理想是指路明灯。没有理想，就没有坚定的方向；没有方向，就没有生活。

7. If you would go up high, then use your own legs! Do not let yourselves carried aloft; do not seat yourselves on other people's backs and heads .
   如果你想走到高处，就要使用自己的两条腿！不要让别人把你抬到高处；不要坐在别人的背上和头上。

05 Eagle in a Storm
风雨中的雄鹰

Did you know that an eagle knows when a storm is approaching long before it breaks? The eagle will fly to some high spot and wait for the winds to come. When the storm hits, it sets its wings so that the winds will pick it up and **lift** it above the storm. While the storm **rages below**, the eagle is **soaring** above it. The eagle does not escape the storm. It simply uses the storm to lift it higher. It rises on the winds that bring the storm.

When the storms of life come upon us and all of us will experience them, we can rise above them by **setting** our belief that we can make it. The storms do not have to overcome us. We can allow our inner power to lift us above them. We can enable ourselves to ride the winds of the storm that bring sickness, **tragedy**, failure and disappointment in our lives. We can soar above the storm. Remember, it is not the **burdens** of life that weigh us down; it is how we handle them.

你知道在暴风雨来临之前，鹰早就能发觉吗？鹰会飞到一个高点，等待起风。当暴风雨来临的时候，它调整翅膀以至于风能够把它带起来，升高到暴风雨的上面。暴风雨在下面肆虐，鹰就在上面翱翔。鹰并没有躲过暴风雨，它只是利用暴风雨使自身升高。它飞到了气流的上面。

当生活中的暴风雨降临，我们人人都要经历的时候，我们也可以通过建立我们能够成功的信念来驾驭这些苦难。困难不一定要击垮我们。我们可以让我们内心的力量来帮助自己去驾驭困难。我们能够去驾驭那些给我们的生活带来疾病、灾难、失败和沮丧的暴风雨。我们可以在风雨之上翱翔。切记，让我们疲惫不堪的并不是生活的重担，而是我们处理困难的方式。

单词解析 Word Analysis

lift [lɪft] *vt.* 举起；运送；偷窃；升高；还清；取消

例 He was too weak even to lift his hand.
他虚弱得连手都抬不起来。

rage [reɪdʒ] *v.* 大怒；怒斥；激烈进行；肆虐

例 That is why the storms rage so fiercely on the sea.
这就是海上刮起这样凶猛的暴风的原因。

below [bɪ'loʊ] *adv.* 在下面；向下

例 The information below was compiled by our correspondent.
以下资料是我们的记者收集整理的。

soar [sɔːr] *vi.* 翱翔；高飞；猛增；高涨；高耸

例 The eagle can soar without flapping their wings.
老鹰无需振翼就能翱翔。

set [set] *vt.* 放置；设定；确定；规定；调整；分配；（太阳）落下去

例 How do we set the enrollment criteria?
我们如何设定录取标准？

tragedy ['trædʒədi] *n.* 悲剧；灾难；惨事

例 Tragedy is in store for that poor girl from the beginning.
从一开始，那个女孩的悲剧就是不可避免的。

burden ['bɜːrdn] *n.* 负担；责任；装载量；主题；[音乐]副歌

例 The burden on his back seemed to be crushing him to the earth.
他背上的重负似乎要把他压倒在地。

语法知识点 Grammar Points

① **When the storm hits, it sets its wings so that the wind will pick it up and lift it above the storm.**

这个句子中，开头是when引导的时间状语从句，之后是so that引导的目的状语从句，表示"it sets its wings"的目的。

例 We turned on the light so that we might see (=so as to see) what it was.
我们把灯打开，以便看看它是什么。
Bring it closer so that I may see it better.
把它拿近点儿，让我仔细看看。
They put a screen around his bed so that the doctor could examine him.
他们在他床的四周放上屏风，以便医生给他检查。

pick up 是固定搭配，表示"捡起；收集；继续；得到；接人；偶然结识；站起，扶起；学会；逮捕；振作精神"

例 He picked up the child and put her on his shoulders.
他抱起孩子让她骑在自己的肩膀上。
He picked up news from all sources.
他从各种渠道收集消息。
She's living with a man she picked up on holiday.
她与一个在假日认识的男人同住。

② **When the storms of life come upon us and all of us will experience them we can rise above them by setting our belief that we can make it.**

这个句子中，前面是when引导的时间状语从句，最后一部分是that引导的同位语，先行词是belief，从句是对belief的解释说明，that在从句中不做任何成分。

例 The news that our school team won the game excited us.
我们校队赢了比赛的消息令我们非常振奋。

③ **We can enable ourselves to ride the winds of the storm that bring sickness, tragedy, failure and disappointment in our lives.**

这个句子中，enable sb. to do sth. 表示能够让某人干某事

例 This pass enables me to travel half-price on trains.
我用这张通行证可以半价乘火车旅行。
He invented a machine to enable people in wheelchairs to get up stairs.
他发明了一个机器可以使坐在轮椅上的人上楼梯。

Eagle in a Storm
风雨中的雄鹰 05

后面是that引导的定语从句，先行词是the winds of the storm，that 在从句中做主语。

> ④ **Remember, it is not the burdens of life that weigh us down; it is how we handle them.**

这个句子是个强调句，结构为"it is ...+that ..."，把这一结构去掉后句子仍完整。

例 It is the book that helps me to learn cooking.
这本书帮我学做饭。

weigh down 使……负重担；使疲惫不堪；使沉重

例 Jane weighed down her repertory with these plays.
这几出戏使简的演出剧目得到了加强。

经典名句 Famous Classics

1. It is at our mother's knee that we acquire our noblest and truest and highest, but there is seldom any money in them.
   人们通常在小的时候拥有最高尚、最真诚和最远大的理想，但这些理想往往赚不到钱。

2. He is a fine friend. He stabs you in the front.
   在你面前攻击你的人，往往是你的好朋友。

3. Living without an aim is like sailing without a compass.
   生活没有目标就像航海没有指南针。

4. It is important to our friends to believe that we are unreservedly frank with them, and important to friendship that we are not.
   对朋友们来说，知道我们对他们坦诚以待是非常重要的；而对友谊来说，同样重要的是，不要真的对他们事事相告。

5. The man with a new idea is a crank until the idea succeeds.
   具有新想法的人在其想法实现之前是个怪人。

6. Fan the sinking flame of hilarity with the wing of friendship; and pass the rosy wine.
   让友谊的翅膀煽起逐渐熄灭的欢乐的火苗；把红酒拿上桌来吧。

7. The ideals which have lighted my way, and time after time have given me new courage to face life cheerfully have been kindness, beauty and truth .

有些理想曾为我们引过道路,并不断给我新的勇气以欣然面对人生,那些理想就是——真、善、美。

06 Keep the Trolls Away from Your Goals
笼中之蟹

There is a type of **crab** that cannot be caught. It is **agile** and clever enough to get out of any crab trap. And yet, these crabs are caught by the thousands every day, thanks to a particular human **trait** they possess. The trap is a wire cage with a hole at the top. **Bait** is placed in the cage, and the cage is lowered into the water. One crab comes along, enters the cage, and begins **munching** on the bait. A second crab joins him. A third. Crab Thanksgiving. Eventually, however, all the bait is gone. The crabs could easily climb up the side of the cage and through the hole, but they do not. They stay in the cage. Other crabs come along and join them long after the bait is gone. And more. Should one of the crabs realize there is no further reason to stay in the trap and attempt to leave, the other crabs will gang up on him and stop him. They will repeatedly pull him off the side of the cage. If he is **persistent**, the others will tear off his claws to keep him from climbing. If he persists still, they will kill him. The crabs "by force of the majority" stay together in the cage. The cage is **hauled up**, and it's dinner

有一种抓不到的蟹。它非常灵活、聪明，能从任何捕蟹笼里逃出来。但是，由于人类拥有的一项特殊技能，每天能抓到成千上万只这种蟹。用的陷阱是一个顶部有洞的金属笼子。把诱饵放在笼子里，然后把笼子沉到水中。一只蟹爬了过来，进到了笼子里，开始吃诱饵。第二只蟹加入了它。然后第三只。就像蟹的感恩节。最后，所有的诱饵都没了。这些蟹本可以轻易地沿着笼子的一边通过那个洞，但是它们没有。它们仍然待在笼子里。在诱饵被吃完很久之后，还是有其他的蟹爬过来加入它们。然后越来越多的蟹加入。如果其中有一只蟹意识到没有理由再待在笼子里了，并试图离开的时候，其他的蟹就会攻击他阻止他，会不断地把它从笼子壁上拉下来。如果它坚持，其他的蟹会为了不让它爬而扯掉它的爪子。如果它还是坚持，它们会杀了它。"在大多数蟹的逼迫下"，这些蟹一起待在笼子里。笼子被提起，码头上的人

time on the **pier**. The chief difference between these crabs and humans is that these crabs live in water and humans on land. Anyone who has a dream "—one that might get them out of what they perceive to be a trap" had best beware of the fellow-**inhabitants** of the trap. The human crabs (we call them **trolls**) do not usually use physical force although they are certainly not above it. They generally don't need it, however. They have more effective methods at hand and in mouth. Doubt, **ridicule**, sarcasm, humiliation and dozen others not listed in our dictionary. The point is to manage to keep the trolls away from your goals.

们准备吃晚餐。这些蟹和人类主要的区别是蟹生活在水里，而人类生活在陆地上。任何梦想"带领大家逃出险境的领路者"必定对险境里的伙伴有着最深的了解。人类中的蟹，即怪人，一般不使用武力，虽然他们也没有高级到哪去。他们一般不需要武力。它们有更有效的方法，那就是用嘴巴——怀疑、嘲笑、讽刺、侮辱，还有许多没有列出来的方式。我要说的就是不要让这些恶夫阻挡了你追求目标的道路。

单词解析 Word Analysis

crab [kræb] *n.* 蟹；阴虱；爱争吵的人；[植]山楂

例 All the shops on the seafront had crab for sale.
海滨地区的全部商店都出售蟹。

agile ['ædʒl] *adj.* （动作）敏捷的；灵活的；（头脑）机灵的

例 One needs an agile mind to solve puzzles.
解谜必须有机灵的头脑。

trait [treɪt] *n.* 特征，特点；少许；一笔

例 One of his less attractive traits is criticizing his wife in public.
他有个不大讨人喜欢的特点，就是爱当众责备妻子。

bait [beɪt] *n.* 饵；引诱

例 Earth worms are often used as bait.
蚯蚓常用作鱼饵。

Keep the Trolls Away from Your Goals
笼中之蟹

munch [mʌntʃ] *v.* 大声咀嚼

例 Munching the apple as he was, he had an eye for all her movements.
他虽然啃着苹果，但却留神地监视着她的每一个动作。

persistent [pərˈsɪstənt] *adj.* 坚持的；连续的；固执的

例 His great success cannot depart from his persistent effort.
他取得这么大的成功和他坚持不懈的努力分不开。

haul up 举起；使船头更近风向；迎风行驶

例 The boat's going off course, and we'll have to haul up.
船要偏离航线了，我们得转向迎风行驶。

pier [pɪr] *n.* 码头；桥墩；桥柱

例 Takings at the pier have dropped off this season.
这个季节，码头上的收入下降了。

inhabitant [ɪnˈhæbɪtənt] *n.* 居民

例 Every inhabitant here has an obligation to pay taxes.
这里的每一位居民都有纳税的义务。

troll [troʊl] *n.* 山精；巨怪 *v.* 闲逛

例 With the key, you can free the imprisoned trolls.
用这把钥匙，你可以释放被囚禁的巨人们。

ridicule [ˈrɪdɪkjuːl] *n.* 嘲笑；愚弄；笑柄

例 Her conduct subjected her to public ridicule.
她的行为使她受众人嘲笑。

语法知识点 Grammar Points

① **Should one of the crabs realize there is no further reason to stay in the trap and attempt to leave, the other crabs will gang up on him and stop him.**

这个句子用了虚拟语气。原句应该是：If one of the crabs should realize there is no further reason to stay in the trap and attempt to leave, the other crabs

will gang up on him and stop him. should提前，省略了if. 表示与将来相反。
虚拟语气在条件从句中的应用。条件从句通常用if来引导，构成形式如下：

与现在相反：从句用if……+动词过去式，主句用would+动词原形。

例 If she had more money, she would dress more fashionably.
如果她有更多的钱，她会打扮得更加时尚。

与过去相反：从句用if……+had+动词过去分词，主句用would have+过去分词。

例 If I had known her phone number, I would have called her.
如果我早就知道她的电话号码，我之前就打给她了。

与将来相反：

a. 从句用if+动词过去式，主句用would+动词原形。

例 If you asked me tomorrow, I would be able to give you the answer.
如果你明天问我，我会给你答案。

b. 从句用if+were to，主句用would+动词原形。

例 If the sun were to rise in the west, I would lend you the money.
如果太阳打西边出来，我就把钱借给你。

c. 从句用if+should，主句用would+动词原形 /祈使句。

例 If he should be sick, he would send for the doctor.
如果他生病了，他会派人去请医生。

例 If you should come tomorrow, please take your notebook.
如果你明天来，请带着你的笔记本。

注意：If+had+动词过去分词，可以省略if 把had 提前，其他成分保持原位。Should 亦可提前，省略if。

gang up on sb. 对付某人，制止某人

例 The victim had no chance when four or five thugs ganged up on him.
当四五个暴徒联合起来攻击那个受害者时，受害人就没有任何反抗的机会了。

② **If he is persistent, the others will tear off his claws to keep him from climbing.**

这个句子也是条件状语从句，从句中if 加一般现在式，主句中用将来时。

tear off 撕掉；匆匆离开

例 Tear off the rhetorical top dressing from his speech and you find there's very little solid content.
去掉他演讲中华丽的辞藻，你会发现其中没什么实在内容。

keep sb./sth. from sth./v.-ing 阻止；免于

例 Please keep the children from swimming in the sea. There are some dangerous currents just off the shore.
请不要让孩子们在海里游泳，岸边也有一些危险的水流。

The government is considering further action to keep the pound from falling in value.
政府正在考虑采取进一步措施避免英镑贬值。

What shall I do to keep this from getting dirty?
我该怎么办才能使它免遭污染?

经典名句 Famous Classics

1. The only limit to our realization of tomorrow will be our doubts of today.
   实现明天理想的唯一障碍是今天的疑虑。

2. Friendship is a disinterested commerce between equals; love, an abject intercourse between tyrants and slaves.
   友谊是平等的人们之间无利益纠葛的来往；而爱情总是发号施令的一方与被奴役的一方之间可悲的交易。

3. An open foe may prove a curse. But a pretended friend is worse.
   虽然你公开的敌人会咒骂并加害于你，但是假装是你的朋友的人更加可怕。

4. You shall judge of a man by his foes as well as by his friends.
   要评价一个人，既要看他的朋友，也要看他的敌人。

5. When an end is lawful and obligatory, the indispensable means to be also lawful and obligatory.
   如果一个目的是正当而必须做的，则达到这个目的的必要手段也是正当而必须采取的。

6. A man can do is make a good example, to have the courage to hold in the social ethical beliefs groundless talk.
一个人所能做的就是做出好榜样，要有勇气在风言风语的社会中坚定地高举伦理的信念。

7. Learning knowledge should be good at thinking, thinking, and thinking. That's how I became a scientist.
学习知识要善于思考，思考，再思考。我就是靠这个方法成为科学家的。

读书笔记

07 Sure You Can
相信自己

Remember when you were a little child trying to learn to walk? First you had to learn to stand: a process involving constantly falling down, and then getting back up. You laughed sometimes and cried at other times. Somehow there was a determination and **conviction** that you would succeed, no matter what. After much practice you finally figured out how to balance yourself, a necessary requirement. You enjoyed this new feeling of power-you'd stand everywhere you could in your **crib**, by the **couch**. It was a **joyous** time you did it! You were in control of you. Now "the next step" walking. You'd seen others do it — "it didn't look that hard"—just move your legs while you were standing. Wrong – more **complexity** than you ever imagined. More frustration than anyone should have to deal with. But you tried, again and again and again until you figured this out. If people caught you walking, they applauded, they laughed, it was, "Oh my God, look at what he's/she's doing." This encouragement **fueled** you on; it raised your self-confidence.

还记得你小时候刚开始学着走路吗？首先得学会站立，这是一个不断摔倒又站起来的过程。有时候会笑，有时候也会哭。不知为何，总有一种一定会成功的决心和信念。在经过多次练习之后你终于明白怎样保持自身平衡，这也是一个必要的需求。在婴儿床上，在沙发旁，你很享受这种想站在哪就站在哪的感觉。那确实是一段充满欢乐的时光！你能控制自己。接下来的一步是走路。你看到别人走的时候没有那么难，只是站着然后动腿。大错特错，走路要远比你想象的复杂。所以你比任何人都沮丧。但是你一遍又一遍地尝试，直到你学会走路。如果你走路的时候别人在场，他们会鼓掌，会笑，好像在说："太棒了，看他/她呀！"这种鼓舞激励你前进，并增强你的自信心。但又有多少次，在你尝试走路的时候，没有人在旁边看着你，鼓励你，你不能等着别人鼓励才走下一步。你学着自我鼓励。如果现在我们还

But how many times did you attempt when no one was watching, when no one was cheering? You couldn't wait for someone to encourage you to take the next steps. You learned how to encourage yourself. If we could only remember this about ourselves today, remember that we can do anything we set our minds to if we are willing to go through the process, just like when we learned to walk. We don't need to wait for others to encourage us; we need to encourage ourselves. If you've forgotten how to do this, or feel like your self-esteem needs a **boost**, take a short journey back through your life— "look at your accomplishments, no matter if they were large or small, " You met the challenge and figured out a way to succeed.

While going back, look for the little child you once were. Thank them for never giving up. As you wave goodbye, remember they will never give up on you. They have believed in you all of your life! Now you need to believe in you, too! Remember, today is the best day of your life because yesterday was and tomorrow may only be.

能记得这些事情，记得为了克服困难我们可以支配自己的思想做一些工作，就像我们学走路一样。我们不需要等待别人的鼓励，我们需要自我鼓励。如果你不记得怎么去做，或是觉得你的自尊心需要加强，那就回顾一下你的人生，看看你那些或大或小的成就，那时你遇到挑战，总会找到通往成功的道路。

回顾的时候，找到曾经的那个小小的你。谢谢他不曾放弃。当你向他告别的时候，也要记得他永远不会放弃你。他一直相信你，相信你的人生！现在你也需要对自己有信心！记住，昨天曾经是，明天可能是，今天确实是你人生中最美好的一天。

单词解析 Word Analysis

conviction [kən'vɪkʃn] *n.* 坚信；定罪；信服
例 She holds deep religious convictions.
她有深刻的宗教信仰。

crib [krɪb] *n.* 婴儿小床；食槽
例 Walk softly as you approach the baby's crib.
当你走近婴儿小床时，步子轻一点。

couch [kaʊtʃ] *n.* 长椅；睡椅；长沙发；兽穴
例 Little Tom was lolling about on the couch, eating sweets.
小汤姆懒洋洋地躺在睡椅上，吃着糖果。

joyous ['dʒɔɪəs] *adj.* 充满快乐的；使人高兴的
例 The poem is a joyous affirmation of the power of love.
这首诗以欢快的笔触肯定了爱情的力量。

complexity [kəm'pleksəti] *n.* 复杂；复杂性；复杂的事物
例 I often reflect on the beauty and complexity of life.
我们经常思考人生的美丽与复杂。

fuel ['fjuːəl] *vt.* 刺激
例 Higher salaries helped fuel inflation.
提高工资刺激通货膨胀。

boost [buːst] *n.* 增加；推进；鼓励
例 This will be a great boost to the economy.
这对于经济发展将是一个巨大的促进。

语法知识点 Grammar Points

① Somehow there was a determination and conviction that you would succeed, no matter what.

这个句子中有there be结构，尽管后面是"determination and conviction"，但是符合就近原则，所以谓语动词用单数。

例 There is a book, two pencils and some buttons on the table.
在桌子上，有一本书、两支铅笔和一些扣子。

同样符合就近原则的还有用连词either...or, neither...nor, whether...or, not only...but(also), or 等连接的并列主语。

例 Either the boy or the girl knows him well.
这男孩或是那女孩了解他。

Neither money nor fame has influence on me.
钱和荣誉都不会让我动心。

Not only you but also he is wrong.
你和他都错了。

② **Remember that we can do anything we set our minds to if we are willing to go through the process, just like when we learned to walk.**

这个句子中有that 引导的宾语从句，做remember的宾语；if 引导的条件状语从句以及when 引导的时间状语从句。

go through 经历；检查；浏览；通过，穿过；经历，遭受；履行，实行。

例 I've gone through the elbows of my sweater.
我毛衣的肘部都磨破了。

He thought it his duty to go through the papers.
他认为自己有责任检查这些文件。

经典名句 Famous Classics

1. Everyone has a certain ideal, this ideal determines the direction of his efforts and judgment. In this sense, I never bring comfort and happiness as the purpose of life itself — the ethical basis, I call it the ideal pigsty. The ideals which have lighted my way, and time after time have given me new courage to face life cheerfully have been kindness, beauty and truth.

每个人都有一定的理想，这种理想决定着他的努力和判断的方向。在这个意义上，我从来不把安逸和快乐看作是生活目的本身——这种伦理基础，我叫它猪栏式的理想。照亮我的道路，并且不断地给我新的勇气去愉快地正视生活的理想，是善、美和真。

Sure You Can
相信自己 07

2. Men build bridges and throw railroads across deserts, and yet they contend successfully that the job of sewing on a button is beyond them. Accordingly, they don't have to sew buttons.
男人们能够建造桥梁，在荒地建起铁路；而他们同样成功地抗辩说缝扣子超乎他们的能力。所以，男人们不需要缝扣子。

3. A woman, especially, if she have the misfortune of knowing anything, should conceal it as well as she can.
一个女人如果很不幸地是个聪明的人，她就应该把她的智慧隐藏得越深越好。

4. All that you do, do with your might; things done by halves are never done right.
做一切事都应尽力而为，半途而废永远不行。

5. Four short words sum up what has lifted most successful individuals above the crowd: a little bit more.
四个简短的词汇概括了成功的秘诀：多一点点！

6. A pessimist sees the difficulty in every opportunity. An optimist sees the opportunity in every difficulty.
悲观主义者在每一次机遇中看到困难，乐观主义者在每一次困难中看到机遇。

7. The worst way to miss someone is to be seated by his/her side and know you'll never have him/her.
天底下最伤感的莫过于彼此间咫尺天涯的距离。

读书笔记

08 Learn From Failure
从失败中学习

Why are so many people so afraid of failure? Quite simply because no one tells us how to fail so that failure becomes an experience that will lead to **growth**. We forget that failure is part of the human condition and that every person has the right to fail.

Most parents work hard at either preventing failure or protecting their children from the **knowledge** that they have failed. One way is to lower standards. A mother describes her child's **hurriedly**-made table as "perfect"! Even though it couldn't stand on **uneven** (not same in height) legs. Another way is to shift blame. If John fails in science, his teacher is **unfair** or stupid.

The trouble with **failure-prevention** methods is that they leave a child **unequipped** for life in the real world. The young need to learn that no one can be best at everything, that no one can win all the time and that it's possible to enjoy a game even when you don't win. A child who's not invited to a birthday party, who doesn't make the honor roll or the **baseball** team feel terrible, of course. But

为什么这么多人害怕失败呢？原因很简单，从没有人告诉我们如何失败，并且失败是成长过程中必须经历的。我们忘了，失败是人类生存条件的一部分，每个人都有与失败斗争的经历。

许多父母都努力工作，或许是为了避免失败，或许是为了不让自己的孩子知道他们曾经失败过。有一种办法是降低标准。一位母亲说自己孩子匆匆做成的桌子是"完美的"，哪怕这张桌子由于不均衡桌脚的支撑正摇摇欲坠。另一种办法是"嫁祸"，如果约翰考试没过，那他父母就会认为他的老师是不公平的或愚蠢的。

这些防止失败的策略所带来的麻烦是，他们没能使孩子在这个真实的世界里做好独立生活的准备。年轻人需要知道，没有谁能在各方面都做到最好，没有谁总能获胜，即使你没有获胜，你也可以享受这场比赛。一个没有收到生日宴会邀请，没有上光荣榜或者棒球队的孩子，必然会感到很沮

Learn From Failure
从失败中学习 08

parents should not offer a quick comfort prize or say "It doesn't matter" because it does. The young should be allowed to experience disappointment and be helped to **master** it.

Failure is never **pleasurable**. It hurts grown-ups and children exactly alike. But it can make a positive **contribution** to your life once you learn to use it. Step one is to ask "Why did I fail?" Control the natural **impulse** to blame someone else. Ask yourself what you did wrong, and how you can improve. If someone else can help, don't be shy about asking them. Success, which encourages repetition of old behavior, is not nearly as good a teacher as failure. You can learn from a bad party how to give a good one, from an ill-chosen first house what to look for in a second. Even a failure that seems definitive can cause fresh thinking, a change of direction. After twelve years of studying ballet, a friend of mine applied for a professional company. She was turned down. "Would further traning help?" She asked. That ballet master shook his head. "You will never be a dancer," he said, "you haven't the body for it."

In such cases, the way to use failure is to take stock bravely asking "What have I left? What else can I do?" My

丧。父母不应该给他们一个快速安慰奖励，或者是在事实上并不是没关系的情况下说"这都没关系的"。应该允许年轻人经历失望，并且帮助他们控制它。

失败不可能使人愉快。它会伤害到成年人，同样也会伤害到孩子。但是，一旦你学会运用它，它就能对你的生活有积极的贡献。第一步是问："为什么我会失败？"不要受到本性冲动的影响去责备他人。问问自己到底做错了什么，如何才能改进。如果有人帮助你，就不要羞于请教。成功，会激发人们重复自己的行为，根本不会比失败更让人受益良多。你可以从一场糟糕的宴会上学会如何办一场成功的宴会。从第一次失败的选房经历中学会如何寻找第二个。明确的失败甚至会让人涌现出新的想法，改变方向。我的一个朋友在学了12年芭蕾舞之后去了一家专业公司进行面试。她被拒绝了。"我还需要进一步接受培训吗？"她问。芭蕾舞教练摇摇头。"你不可能成为一名舞蹈演员，"他说，"你不是块跳芭蕾舞的料。"

在这样的情况下，利用失败的方法是勇敢地进行自我总结，问问："我还剩下什么？我

friend put away her shoes and moved into dance treatment center, a field where she's both able and useful. Failure frees one to take risks because there's less to lose. Often there is recovery of energy — a way to find new possibilities.

还可以做什么？"我的朋友收好了她的芭蕾舞鞋，然后转而从事舞蹈治疗，这是一个对她来说很在行也很实用的领域。失败可以让人不必再去冒险，因为失败的人几乎没有什么可以再失去的了。通常，失败还会让人精力复苏，认识到一些新的可能性。

单词解析 Word Analysis

growth [grəʊθ] *n.* 生长；增长

例 A steady growth in the popularity of two smaller parties may upset the polls.
两个较小政党的支持率稳步上升，可能会打乱投票结果。

knowledge ['nɒlɪdʒ] *n.* 了解，理解；知识

例 She told Parliament she had no knowledge of the affair.
她告诉议会她对此事并不知情。

hurriedly ['hʌrɪdlɪ] *adv.* 仓促地，匆忙地

例 He tramped hurriedly round the lake towards the garden.
他匆匆地迈着沉重的步伐绕过湖边向花园走去。

uneven [ʌn'iːvn] *adj.* 不平的，一长一短的

例 What kids experience now is an uneven rate of development. They are forced to be older than their years.
小孩子现在的问题是成长速度不均衡。他们被迫变得比自己的实际年龄老成。

unfair [ˌʌn'feə(r)] *adj.* 不公正的，不公平的

例 The American plane makers continue to accuse Airbus of unfair competition.
美国飞机制造商继续指控空中客车公司不正当竞争。

Learn From Failure 08
从失败中学习

failure-prevention [ˈfeɪljə(r)- prɪˈvenʃn] 故障预防

unequipped [ˈʌnɪˈkwɪpt] *adj.* 未配备所需物品的，无准备的

例 The trouble with failure-prevention devices is that they leave a child unequipped for life in the real world.
这种防止失败的策略的问题是使孩子们对现实的世界毫无准备。

baseball [ˈbeɪsbɔːl] *n.* 棒球；[体]棒球运动

例 They were beaten to death with baseball bats.
他们被人用棒球棒打死了。

master [ˈmɑːstə(r)] *vt.* 精通，熟练；征服

例 Jackson remained calm and always master of his passions.
杰克逊镇定自若，始终克制着情绪。

pleasurable [ˈpleʒərəbl] *adj.* 令人快乐的，愉快的，舒适的

例 The most pleasurable experience of the evening was the wonderful fireworks display.
这个晚上最让人高兴的就是精彩的焰火表演。

contribution [ˌkɒntrɪˈbjuːʃn] *n.* 贡献，捐赠，捐助

例 American economists have made important contributions to the field of financial and corporate economics.
美国的经济学家们在金融和企业经济学领域做出了重要的贡献。

impulse [ˈɪmpʌls] *n.* 凭冲动行事；突如其来的念头

例 Unable to resist the impulse, he glanced at the sea again.
他抑制不住冲动，又向海面瞥了一眼。

语法知识点 Grammar Points

① **Quite simply because no one tells us how to fail so that failure becomes an experience that will lead to growth.**

本句中 because 引导原因状语从句，so that 引导结果状语从句，最后一个 that 引导定语从句，先行词 an experience 在从句中做主语；lead to 表示"导致，通向"。

例 A lack of prudence may lead to financial problems.
不够谨慎可能会导致财政上出现问题。

so that 主要引导两种从句：目的状语从句和结果状语从句。

例 My old father began to study computer at the age of sixty so that he might keep up with times.
父亲六十岁时才开始学习电脑，以便跟上时代。（目的状语从句）

She had not planned her time well, so that she did not finish her homework on time.
她没把时间计划好，所以没按时完成家庭作业。（结果状语从句）

② **Most parents work hard at either preventing failure or protecting their children from the knowledge that they have failed.**

本句中 either...or... 表示"要么……要么……"；protect sb. from 表示"保护某人免于"。

例 They gave money to the Conservative Party either personally or through their companies.
他们要么以个人名义要么通过他们的公司捐钱给了保守党。

The most important trees were tagged to protect them from being damaged by construction machinery.
最珍贵的树木都被贴上了标签，以防被建筑机械毁坏。

③ **A child who's not invited to a birthday party, who doesn't make the honor roll or the baseball team feel terrible, of course.**

本句较长，分析出句子的主干 A child feel terrible，句中两个 who 均引导定语从句，先行词在从句中做主语。

④ **But it can make a positive contribution to your life once you learn to use it.**

本句中，once 为连词，引导条件状语从句；once引导的从句不能用将来时，如果谓语动词是将来发生的动作，动词常用一般现在时来代替将来时。

例 Once you begin, you must go on.
一旦开了头，就应该继续下去。

Once you see the film, you will never forget it.
一旦你看了这部电影，你将永远不会忘记。

Learn From Failure 从失败中学习 08

make contribution to 表示"为……做出贡献"。

例 I think this will make contribution to our Jilin educational reform.
我想这对我们吉林的教育改革将会有很大贡献。

Let's work hard to make contribution to our country in the future.
让我们努力工作,为我们的国家做出更大的贡献。

经典名句 Famous Classics

1. A man can fail many times, but he isn't a failure until he begins to blame somebody else.
   一个人可以失败很多次,但是只要他没有开始责怪旁人,他还不是一个失败者。

2. If you have great talents, industry will improve them; if you have but moderate abilities, industry will supply their deficiency.
   如果你很有天赋,勤勉会使其更加完善;如果你能力一般,勤勉会补足其缺陷。

3. Few things are impossible in themselves; and it is often for want of will, rather than of means, that man fails to succeed.
   事情很少有根本做不成的;其所以做不成,与其说是条件不够,不如说是由于决心不够。

4. Dare and the world always yields. If it beats you sometimes, dare it again and again and it will succumb.
   大胆挑战,世界总会让步。如果有时候你被它打败了,不断地挑战,它总会屈服。

5. Ideal are like the stars — we never reach them, but like mariners, we chart our course by them.
   理想犹如天上的星星,我们犹如水手,虽不能达到天上,但是我们的航程可凭借它指引。

6. Health is certainly more valuable than money, because it is by health that money is procured.
   健康当然比金钱更为重要,因为拥有了健康我们才能获得金钱。

09 Summon up Courage
迎接挑战

There were two men both decided to get a horse. One man found a red horse with much spirit. The other chose one more **docile**. They would go riding together every day. It so happened on the **route** they would take around the countryside. There was a **ditch** about eight or nine feet wide. After a time it was apparent that the red horse's spirit could not be shaken. When coming up to this gap in the **trail**, he **hurled** it the first time. Because of the spirit in him, he was quick to respond and jumped it with no problem. Yet the more docile horse would **balk** every time he came to the **edge**. He wasn't sure of the distance; he would stand on the edge **trembling** with **indecision** and doubt because the distance to him looked too great.

Then one day after a while, coming up to the ditch and watching his companion take it with ease, something happened within him—a knowing was born that he could too. So with **agility** and ease he gracefully **bounded** over the barrier.

Life is much like the two horses. When we as people come up against

有两个人都想要一匹马。一个人找到了一匹红色的性子很烈的马，另一个人则选了一匹温顺的。他们每天都会一起骑马。在他们绕着乡村走的路上有一条大概八九英尺宽的沟，一段时间后，显然对那匹红色的马来说，就完全不能造成阻碍了。在路上靠近这条沟的时候，它第一次就用力地跳了过去。因为它的士气很强，所以它反应非常快，跳过去完全没有问题。但是那匹较温顺的马每次靠近沟都会退缩。它不确定距离是多少，它会站在边缘处犹豫着，颤抖着，因为对它来说那个距离太长了。

之后有一天，它又来到那条沟那儿，看到它的同伴轻松地跳了过去，它心中浮现出了一个想法：我也可以跳过去的。果然它优美地跳过了这道障碍，既灵活又轻松。

生活非常像这两匹马。当我们突然遇到小坑洼或类似的情况时，我们觉得我们不可能越过这段距离，或者距离太长了，我们不确定是否能成功，

trials or situations, we just don't feel like we can make the distance or that it just is too big and we don't know if we'll make it, we balk standing on the edge trembling. It's not until we depend upon the spirit within. Then we are able to make it with ease. Until we quit looking at the **obstacle** or trial through our eyes, they will always seem too big for us. But there is a spirit within us that can judge the distance to the other side and will give us the strength to make it through it. As long as we let it. It all comes to a choice whether we look for the spirit within or just stand on the edge and balk.

所以我们退缩了，站在边缘不住地颤抖。直到我们依靠内心的勇气战胜困难。然后我们就能轻松地成功。直到我们不再通过眼睛去看那些障碍或小坑洼，它们看起来还是很艰难。但是我们心中有一股精神可以衡量到另一边的距离，给我们力量去完成。只要我们让它发挥作用。我们是寻找内心的勇气还是仅仅站在边缘保持退缩，这都是我们的选择。

单词解析 Word Analysis

docile ['dɑ:sl] *adj.* 容易控制的；温顺的

例 He trembled lest he himself should lose a docile pupil.
他担心自己会失去一个听话的学生。

route [ru:t] *n.* 路线；（固定）线路；途径

例 The route was once much travelled but has fallen into disuse.
这条路线旅行的人以前常走，但是现在已不用了。

ditch [dɪtʃ] *n.* 沟渠；壕沟

例 The car ran off the road into a ditch.
汽车驶离道路跌进沟中。

trail [treɪl] *n.* 踪迹；小径；尾；一系列

例 The dogs found the trail of the rabbit.
猎狗发现了兔子的踪迹。

hurl [hɜːrl] *v.* 用力投掷；愤慨地说出；丢下
- 例 The hunter hurled his spear at the tiger.
  猎人用力把他的长矛向虎投去。

balk [bɔːk] *v.* 阻止；突然停止；退缩；拒绝
- 例 Professor Xu says successful sportspeople should not balk at turning over half of their earnings.
  徐教授表示，功成名就的运动员不应拒绝上缴一半的收入。

edge [edʒ] *n.* 边缘；优势；边；刀口
- 例 New houses have mushroomed on the edge of the town.
  城市边缘的新建房屋犹如雨后春笋。

tremble ['trembl] *v.* 发抖；忧虑；震颤
- 例 He was trembling with rage.
  他气得发抖。

indecision [ˌɪndɪˈsɪʒn] *n.* 优柔寡断；无决断力；犹豫不决
- 例 He stood outside the door in an agony of indecision.
  他站在门外，不知如何是好，非常难受。

agility [əˈdʒɪləti] *n.* 敏捷；灵活；轻快
- 例 The boy came upstairs with agility.
  那男孩敏捷地走上楼来。

bound [baʊnd] *vi.* 跳；跳跃前进；猛涨
- 例 Polly came bounding into the room holding a letter.
  波利手上拿着一封信，蹦蹦跳跳地跑进了房间。

obstacle [ˈɑːbstəkl] *n.* 障碍；绊脚石
- 例 Lack of education is an obstacle of success.
  缺乏教育是成功的障碍。

语法知识点 *Grammar Points*

① He wasn't sure of the distance; he would stand on the edge trembling with indecision and doubt because the distance to him looked too great.

be sure of 确信

be sure of oneself 自信

例 He's not so sure of himself these days.
他近来不大有自信。

on the edge 在边缘上；坐立不安

例 The factory is situated on the edge of the town.
这座工厂坐落在该城的边上。

The diver poised on the edge of the high board.
跳水运动员在高台边上站稳。

trembling with indecision and doubt是现在分词做伴随状语，he和trembling是主谓关系。

② Then one day after a while, coming up to the ditch and watching his companion take it with ease, something happened within him, a knowing was born that he could too.

after a while 过一会儿；不久

例 After a while, these people cooled off towards me.
过了一会儿，这些人对我态度冷淡了。

这个句子中，coming和watching都是现在分词做伴随状语，he与这两个词都是主谓关系。

with ease 容易地；不费力地

例 The horse negotiated the fence with ease.
那马轻易跳过了栅栏。

He passed the test with ease.
他轻而易举地考及格了。

最后一部分是一个同位语从句，先行词是a knowing，从句部分是对a knowing的解释说明，that在从句中不充当任何成分。

③ When we as people come up against trials or situations we just don't feel like we can make the distance or that it just is too big and we don't know if we'll make it, we balk standing on the edge trembling.

这个句子中有when引导的时间状语从句和that引导的宾语从句。

come up against 突然（或意外）碰到（困难、反对等）

> He often came up against the problem of money.
> 他那时常常碰到钱的问题。

feel like 想要

> Do you feel like a game of tennis?
> 你想打一场网球吗？
>
> Do you feel like going to a movie?
> 你想看电影吗？

make it 成功达到预定目标，幸存

> The train goes at 10:15. I think we shall make it.
> 火车10点1刻开，我想我们能赶上。

经典名句 *Famous Classics*

1. Don't forget, a person's greatest emotional need is to feel appreciated.
   不要忘记，一个人最重要的精神需求是得到他人的欣赏。

2. It doesn't matter what others think of you, what matters most is how you see yourself.
   不要太在意别人如何看待你，最为重要的是你如何看待你自己。

3. Don't give up when you still have something to give. Nothing is really over until the moment you stop trying.
   当你还有资本的时候别轻易放弃，只要你自己不停止努力，一切就不会真正结束。

4. Don't set your goals by what other people deem important. Only your know what is best for you.
   不要人云亦云地确定自己的目标，只有你自己知道，对你来说什么是最棒的。

5. Never stop smiling, not even when you're sad, someone might fall in love with your smile.
   永远都不要停止微笑，即使是在你难过的时候，说不定有人会因为你的笑容而爱上你。

6. Don't be afraid to learn. Knowledge is a weightless treasure you can always carry easily.
   不要害怕学习，知识是无法衡量价值的珍宝，拥有了它，你便能轻松上路。

读书笔记

10 Up to You
快乐与痛苦

Jerry was the kind of guy who was always in a good mood and always had something positive to say. One day I went up to Jerry and asked him, "I don't get it! You can't be a positive person all of the time. How do you do it?" Jerry replied, "Each morning I wake up and say to myself, 'Jerry, you have two choices today. You can choose to be in a good mood or you can choose to be in a bad mood.' I choose to be in a good mood." "Yeah, right, it's not that easy, " I **protested**. "Yes it is, " Jerry said. "Life is all about choices. You choose how you **react** to situations. You choose how people will affect your mood. You choose to be in a good mood or bad mood. It's your choice how you live life." I **reflected on** what Jerry said. Soon **thereafter**, I changed my job. We lost touch.

Several years later, I heard that Jerry was **robbed** and was shot. I saw Jerry about six months after the accident. When I asked him how he was, he replied, "I feel really good." I asked him what had gone through his mind when he was taken to the hospital. Jerry replied, "The first thing came to my mind was that I

杰瑞是那种总是很快乐、总是传递正能量的男孩。一天我去找他，然后问他："我不明白！你不可能一直都很快乐啊。你是怎么做到的？"杰瑞回答道："每天早晨我醒来后，都会对自己说，杰瑞，你今天有两个选择：快乐或痛苦。我会选择快乐。"我反对道："是，是那样，但是没那么简单啊。"杰瑞又说："生活全部都是选择。你选择如何对所处环境做出反应。你选择身边的人们怎样影响你的情绪。你选择保持快乐或是痛苦。如何生活也是你的选择。"我思考着杰瑞说的话。在那之后不久，我换了工作。我们就失去了联系。

多年以后，我听说杰瑞遭遇了抢劫，还被子弹击中了。意外后大概六个月的时候我见到了杰瑞。我问他最近怎么样，他回答道："我挺好的。"我又问他当他被送往医院的时候，他在想些什么，他回答道："我首先想到的就是我本应该关上后门的。然后我

should have closed the back door. Then I remembered that I had two choices: I could choose to live, or I could choose to die. I chose to live." Jerry continued, "The nurses kept telling me I was going to be fine. But when they **wheeled** me into the **emergency** room and the expressions on the faces of the doctors and nurses scared me. In their eyes, I read, 'He's a dead man.' I knew I needed to take action. "What did you do?" I asked. "Well, a nurse asked if I was **allergic** to anything," said Jerry, "Yes" I replied. The doctors and nurses were waiting for my reply... I took a deep breath and yelled, "Bullets!" Over their laughter, I told them, "I am choosing to live. Operate on me as if I am alive, not dead." Jerry lived thanks to the skill of his doctors, but also because of his amazing attitude. I learned from him that every day we have the choice to live positively.

又想起我有两个选择：活下去或者死亡。然后我选择了活下去。"杰瑞继续说道："当时护士一直跟我说我一定会没事的。但是当她们把我推进急救室的时候，医生和护士们脸上的表情把我吓坏了。从他们的眼睛里，我看到好像在说，他是个死人。那时我知道我必须采取行动了。""你做了什么？"我问。杰瑞说："一个护士问我有没有对什么东西过敏，然后我回答有。医生和护士们等着我的答复……我深呼吸了一下，大喊道，子弹！在他们的笑声中，我告诉他们，我想要活下去，给我做手术吧。"多亏医生的医术高明，也是因为杰瑞积极的生活态度，他活了下来。我从他身上学会了，每天我们都有选择快乐地生活的权利。

单词解析 Word Analysis

protest ['prəutest] 抗议；反对；申明；断言

例 They protested to the mayor that the taxes were too high.
他们向市长提出抗议说税款过高。

react [ri'ækt] 反应；反攻

例 Iron reacts with water and air to produce rust.
铁与水和空气起化学反应而生锈。

reflect [rɪˈflekt] *v.* 反映；反射；反省；归咎；显示

例 Her sad looks reflected the thought passing through her mind.
她忧戚的面容反映出她内心的思想。

reflect on 考虑；反思

例 I always reflect on life when listening to Beethoven's symphony.
每当听贝多芬交响乐的时候，我总会仔细思考人生。

thereafter [ˌðerˈæftər] *adv.* 其后；从那时以后

例 Thereafter his idea of attending school gradually strengthened.
其后他求学的信念逐渐增强。

rob [rɑːb] *v.* 抢劫；掠夺

例 Not only do they rob you, but also they smash everything.
他们不仅抢夺你的财物，还要把每样东西都捣毁。

wheel [wiːl] *vt.* 用车运；转动；给……装轮子

例 Will you wheel him away because he can't walk?
他不能走路，你把他推走好吗？

emergency [iˈmɜːrdʒənsi] *adj.* 应急的；紧急的；备用的

例 There are four emergency exits in the department store.
这家百货公司有四个紧急出口。

allergic [əˈlɜːrdʒɪk] *adj.* 过敏的；反感的

例 Nuts can trigger off a violent allergic reaction.
坚果可以引起严重的过敏反应。

语法知识点 Grammar Points

① I reflected on what Jerry said.

这是一个what引导的宾语从句，从句做reflected on 的宾语，what在从句中做宾语成分。

reflect有以下几个固定搭配：
(1) reflect back 反射；把……如实地反映出来

> The sea reflected back the bright sunlight.
> 大海反射出明亮的阳光。
> The election results do not always reflect back the views of the voters.
> 选举的结果并不总是真实地反映出选民的观点。

(2) reflect from 从……反射出来

reflect from sth

> The light reflected from the water into my eyes.
> 光线从水面反射进我的双眼。

reflect sth from sth 用于 be ~ ed 结构

> The light is reflected from the moon.
> 光从月球反射回来。

(3) reflect on (upon)

a. 仔细想；回忆

> I have been reflecting on all he said to me.
> 我仔细考虑他对我所说的一切。
> Mr. Smith stood reflecting on the circumstances of the preceding hours.
> 史密斯先生站在那里仔细想着在此之前几个小时的情况。

b. 影响……的荣誉；使……丢脸 reflect on (upon) sb/oneself/sth

> Your rude behaviour reflects only upon yourself.
> 你的粗鲁行为只会损及你自己的名誉。
> Failure to pay your bills reflects on your credit rating.
> 不付账有损你的信用度。

c. 怀疑

> I don't wish to reflect upon your sincerity.
> 我不希望怀疑你的诚意。
> A gentleman should never reflect on another person's motives unless he has good reason for doing so.
> 绅士绝不应该怀疑别人的动机，除非他有足够的理由这样做。

② **I asked him what had gone through his mind when he was taken to the hospital.**

这个句子中有一个what引导的宾语从句和一个when引导的时间状语从句。
go through 经历；检查；浏览；通过；穿过；实行

例 I had a browse through the books on her shelf.
我浏览了一下她书架上的书。

③ The first thing came to my mind was that I should have closed the back door.

这个句子中，came to my mind做The first thing的定语，句子主干是The first thing was that...。
should have done 本应该做某事却没做

例 You should have told me that thing.
你本应该告诉我那件事的。

shouldn't have done 本不应该做某事却做了

例 You shouldn't have used her things without permission.
你本不应该在未经允许的状况下用她的东西的。

④ Jerry lived thanks to the skill of his doctors, but also because of his amazing attitude.

这个句子中thanks to和because of后面的部分做原因状语。近义词还有：due to 因为，由于 owing to 由于。

经典名句 Famous Classics

1. Lies run sprints but the truth runs marathons.
   谎言就像是百米短跑，而真相就像是马拉松赛跑。

2. Try to make at least three people smile each day.
   试着每天至少让三个人微笑。

3. Love makes people forget about time, while time makes people forget about love. Don't let yesterday take up more of today.
   爱情使人忘记时间，时间也使人忘记爱情。不要让太多昨天占据你的今天！

4. Life is a profound book. Other's notes cannot replace your own understanding. May you find and create something new in it.

生活是一本精深的书，别人的注释代替不了自己的理解。愿你有所发现，有所创造。

5. No one can change a person, but someone can be a reason for that person to change.
没人能够改变另一个人，但却能成为别人改变的一个原因。

6. Maybe God wants you to meet many wrong people before you meet the right one, so when this happens, you'll be thankful.
也许上帝让你在遇见那个适合的人之前遇见很多错误的人，所以，当这一切发生的时候，你应该心存感激。

7. For we lose not only by death, but also by leaving and being left, by changing and letting go and moving on.
让我们失去所拥有的不仅仅是死亡，还有离别和离去，以及改变、放弃和前行。

读书笔记

11 You'll Get Exactly What You Expect
期望值

I remember a young lady who went to work for a company immediately after graduating from college. She seemed extremely talented but unbelievably **timid**. She was assigned to a division-level marketing department where she assisted in the production of advertising. Her supervisor associated her shyness with a lack of technical and **conceptual** skills. As a result, she was never included in brainstorming or planning sessions. The **supervisor** thought she was best suited to simple **graphics layout** and **paste-up**. Frustrated that her talents were **squandered** on simple tasks, she applied to the corporate marketing department. The vice-president reviewed her resume and transferred her without interviewing her at length. His concept of the young lady was positive and assigned her to a series of important, key projects. She performed **magnificently**. A few months later, the original supervisor was in the vice-president's office admiring the new corporate ad campaign. The supervisor asked, "What kind of a rain-maker worked this kind of magic?" The VP

我记得有一个年轻的女孩，在大学毕业后立刻去了一家公司工作。她非常有天赋，但却很内向。她被派去了市场部协助宣传产品。她的主管认为她的内向跟缺乏技术上和概念上的技巧有关。所以，她从不参与头脑风暴和做计划的部分。主管觉得她最适合做一些简单的绘图设计和杂事。她的天赋只能浪费在简单的工作上，这让她十分沮丧，所以她申请去企业市场部。副总裁看了她的简历后，没有复杂的面试，就直接把她调了过来。他对这个年轻女孩的印象非常好，任命她做一系列重要的工作。她也表现得非常好。几个月之后，之前的那个主管在副总裁办公室里欣赏新的企业广告宣传。主管问："是谁创造了这种魔力？"副总裁回答道："这都是你派到我这儿的那个女孩子的功劳。这是我做过的最好的决定！"

这只是众多例子中我能列举的其中一个，他们由于过低的不正确的期望而难以前

You'll Get Exactly What You Expect
期望值 11

replied, "This was all completed by that young lady you sent me. That was the best move I ever made!"

This is but one example of the dozens of cases I can document where individuals were **literally hobbled** by low or incorrect expectations. In many instances, the mindset of a co-worker or supervisor can restrict an employee's ability to become an excellent performer. This cause-and-effect model applies to all aspects of our lives. The neighbor's young son asked if he could **mow** my yard. I told him I would talk to his dad first. The father said, "I don't think he can handle a mower. I never let him near mine. Go ahead if you like." I assured him I would watch his son closely and be certain he could handle the equipment safely. The boy not only knew how to handle the mower, but did such a good job. I asked him to help each week. His dad was amazed. "I never would have guessed, " he said. "You should have given him a chance, " I suggested.

行。在很多情况下，同事或者领导的态度可以抑制一个员工变得优秀的能力。这种因果关系模型适用于我们生活的各个方面。一次邻居的小男孩问我他能不能帮忙割我院子里的杂草。我告诉他我得先跟他爸谈谈。他爸爸说："我觉得他不会用割草机。我也从来没让他靠近过它。但是如果你想的话就让他做吧。"我向他保证我会看护好他的儿子，确定他能安全地操作机器。结果，那个男孩不但知道怎么操作割草机，而且做得非常好。我每周都会找他帮忙。男孩的爸爸非常吃惊，说："我从来没有想过。"我建议道："你本应该给他一个机会。"

单词解析 Word Analysis

timid ['tɪmɪd] *adj* 胆怯的；害羞的

例 He is a timid boy. It's impossible for him to brawl with anyone.
他是一个胆小的男孩，他不可能和任何人吵架。

conceptual [kən'septʃuəl] *adj.* 概念的

例 We produced it as a conceptual model to imagine a new life style.
我们把它制作成一个概念模型,想象一个新的生活方式。

supervisor ['suːpərvaɪzər] *n.* 监督人;主管人;管理人;督学;检查员;导师

例 As her immediate supervisor for the last two years, I can state that she is a very good secretary.
作为她两年来的直接领导,我可以说她是一位优秀的秘书。

graphics ['græfɪks] *n.* 制图法;绘图学

例 He carefully shields you from difficult diffraction theory and uses advanced computer generated graphics to show you the appearance of each aberration.
他从复杂的衍射理论里,用电脑制图细心地描绘每一幅失常的画面。

layout ['leɪaʊt] *n.* 安排;布局;设计

例 The designer chooses the layout of reinforcement.
设计者选择钢筋布置。

paste-up ['peɪstʌp] *n.* 东拼西凑而成的文章;任何杂凑而成的东西

例 The professor refused the student's paste-up.
教授拒绝接受学生东拼西凑的文章。

squander ['skwɑːndər] *vt.* 浪费;挥霍

例 It's a crime to squander our country's natural resources.
浪费我们国家的自然资源是一种罪恶。

magnificently [mæg'nɪfɪsntli] *adv.* 很好地

例 She affected magnificently not to care.
她装出一点也不在乎的样子。

literally ['lɪtərəli] *adv.* 逐字地;按照字面上地;不夸张地;正确地;简直

例 He translated this article literally.
他一字一句地翻译这篇文章。

You'll Get Exactly What You Expect
期望值

hobble ['hɒbl] v. 蹒跚；跛行

例 The old man hobbled along (the road) with the aid of his stick.
那老汉拄着拐杖一瘸一拐地走着。

mow [moʊ] v. 割（草、麦等）；扫射；扮鬼脸

例 She's been nagging at him to mow the lawn.
她一直在催他去割草坪的杂草。

语法知识点 Grammar Points

① **I remember a young lady who went to work for a company immediately after graduating from college.**

这个句子中有一个who引导的定语从句和一个after引导的时间状语。先行词是a young lady，who引导的定语从句是做a young lady的解释说明，who在从句中做主语。

graduate from 从……毕业

例 He will graduate from the school in May.
他将要在五月份毕业。

② **She was assigned to a division-level marketing department where she assisted in the production of advertising.**

这个句子是where引导的定语从句，先行词是a division-level marketing department。

be assigned to 被分配给；担当者；指派给

例 Jack was assigned to the assembly shop of the factory.
杰克被分配到厂里的装配间工作。

assist in 参加，帮助

例 A person was trained to live in underwater installations and conduct, assist in, or be a subject of scientific research.
训练能在水下装置物中生活并引导、辅助或作为科学研究的对象。

③ **Her supervisor associated her shyness with a lack of technical and conceptual skills.**

associate...with... 把……与……联系起来；与……交友；与……常在一起

例 He associates with all kinds of people.
他常与各种人交朋友。

I don't associate the two ideas.
这两个概念我联系不起来。

with a lack of 缺乏

例 The news was greeted with a lack of enthusiasm by those at the meeting.
与会者对这消息未表现出多少兴趣。

Critics charged the writer with a lack of originality.
评论家指责这位作家缺少独创性。

④ **Frustrated that her talents were squandered on simple tasks, she applied to the corporate marketing department.**

这个句子中,frustrated做主语she的补语,是对主语的补充说明。

例 She arrived at home at ten o'clock, tired and exhausted.
她晚上十点才到家,筋疲力尽。

squander on 在……上浪费

例 That was quite enough to squander so much money on a rainy night.
一个下雨的夜里浪费这么多钱未免太过分。

She always squanders on clothing.
她总是在购买服装上大手大脚。

apply to 申请;适用于;运用于

例 I advise that they apply to the council for a home improvement grant.
我建议他们向市政会申请改善住房的贷款。

Above terms only apply to dorsa above 3,000 bales.
以上条件,仅适用于三千捆以上的订单。

经典名句 Famous Classics

1. Life is not about being hardworking, diligence and the related struggles, but more about making the right choices.

You'll Get Exactly What You Expect
期望值

人生最困难的不是努力，也不是奋斗，而是做出正确的抉择。

2. Knowing is not enough, we must apply; willing is not enough, we must do.
   仅仅知道是不够的，我们必须应用；仅仅愿意是不够的，我们必须行动。

3. Don't run through life so fast that you forget not only where you've been, but also where you are going .
   不要过于匆忙地走过人生，那样不仅会使你遗忘昨天的轨迹，甚至连目的地都忘记了。

4. You may only be a person in this world, but for someone, you're the world.
   你可能只是这个世界上的一个人，但对于某人来说，你就是全世界。

5. If winter comes, can spring be far behind ?
   冬天来了，春天还会远吗?

6. A man is only as good as what he loves.
   一个人要用他所爱的东西有多好来衡量。

7. Journey of a thousand miles begins with single step.
   千里之行，始于足下。

8. Genius is an infinite capacity for taking pains.
   所谓的天才是不断地承受痛楚。

9. Difficult circumstances serve as a textbook of life for people.
   困难坎坷是人们的生活教科书。

10. The good seaman is known in bad weather.
    惊涛骇浪，方显英雄本色。

读书笔记

12 Hard Work Is Good for Health
努力工作有利健康

Scientists find that the hard-working **prestigious** people live longer than average men and women. Career women are healthier than housewives. Evidences show that the **jobless** are in poorer health than job-holders. An investigation shows that whenever the unemployment rate increases by 1%, the death rate increases **correspondingly** by 2%. All this comes down to one point: work is helpful to health.

Why is work good for health? It is because work keeps people busy, away from loneness and **solitude**. Researches show that people feel unhappy, worried and **solitary** when they have nothing to do. Instead, the happiest are those who are busy. Many high **achievers** who love their careers feel they are most happy when they are working hard. Work serves as a bridge between man and reality. By work, people come into contact with each other. By **collective** activity, they find friendship and **warmth**. This is helpful to health. The loss of work means the loss of everything. It affects man **spiritually** and hence makes him **liable** to disease.

科学家们发现努力工作的名人比一般人寿命长，职业妇女比家庭妇女健康。有证据表明，失业者比在业人员健康状况差。调查表明失业率每增长1%，死亡率相应增长2%。所有这些都表明：工作有利于健康。

为什么工作对健康有好处？因为工作使人忙碌，不会寂寞、孤独。研究表明，人们无事可做时会感到不愉快、忧虑、孤独。忙碌反而使人愉快。许多热爱事业、卓有成就的人在努力工作时感到最幸福。工作可作为人与现实之间的桥梁：通过工作，人们彼此接触；通过集体活动，人们得到友谊和温暖。这有利于健康。失去工作就是失去一切，它影响人的精神，使人容易得病。

此外，工作给人以充实感和成就感。工作使人感到自身的价值和社会地位。作家写完书，医生成功地给病人做完手术，教师看到学生的成长，他们有说不出的幸福。

Hard Work Is Good for Health
努力工作有利健康

Besides, work gives one the sense of **fulfillment** and a sense of achievement. Work makes one feel his value and **status** in society. When a writer finishes his writing or a doctor successfully operates on a patient or a teacher sees his students grow, they are happy beyond words. From the above we can come to the conclusion that the more you work, the happier and healthier you will be.

Let us work hard and study well and live a happy and healthy life.

从以上我们可以得出这一结论：工作越多越幸福，也越健康。

让我们努力工作，好好学习，过幸福健康的生活吧。

单词解析 Word Analysis

prestigious [pre'stɪdʒəs] *adj.* 享有声望的；声望很高的

例 Her first novel won a prestigious literary prize.
她的第一部小说就获得了一个颇具声望的文学奖。

jobless ['dʒɑːbləs] *adj.* 失业的

例 Jobless and penniless, Tom had to sleep rough in the fields for several months.
汤姆没有工作，身无分文，不得不在野外露宿了几个月。

correspondingly [ˌkɒrə'spɒndɪŋlɪ] *adv.* 相应地

例 Correspondingly, the competition is becoming more and more fierce.
相应地，竞争也变得越来越激烈。

solitude ['sɑːlətuːd] *n.* 孤独；独居；荒僻之地；幽静的地方

例 He passed twenty-four years in solitude.
他在孤独中度过了二十四年。

solitary ['sɑːləteri] *adj.* 孤独的；独立的；单个的；唯一的；荒凉的
例 His childhood was repressed and solitary.
他的童年是压抑而孤独的。

achiever [ə'tʃiːvər] *n.* 成功者；有成就的人
例 So we may credit the achiever with brains, brawn or lucky breaks, and let ourselves off the hook because we fall short in all three.
我们也许认为有成就的人聪明，身体健壮或运气好，我们别再自寻烦恼了，因为这三个方面我们都不行。

collective [kə'lektɪv] *adj.* 集体的；共同的
例 They hold together for collective security.
他们为了共同安全而团结在一起。

warmth [wɔːrmθ] *n.* 温暖；热烈；热情；热心
例 The sun gives (us) warmth and light.
太阳供给我们光和热。

spiritually ['spɪrɪtʃuəli] *adv.* 精神上
例 I felt spiritually very depressed.
我精神上感到很压抑。

liable ['laɪəbl] *adj.* 有义务的；应负责的；有……倾向；可能的；易遭受……的，易患……（病）的
例 Parents are liable for children's education.
父母应负责孩子的教育。

fulfillment [fʊl'fɪlmənt] *n.* 满足；完成；履行
例 People find fulfillment in working for a common goal.
人们在为一个共同目标而努力的过程中得到满足。

status ['steɪtəs] *n.* 地位；情形；状况，状态；身份
例 There are many fine shadings of status through the social hierarchy.
在各个社会等级之间有许多细微的身份区别。

Hard Work Is Good for Health
努力工作有利健康

语法知识点 Grammar Points

① **An investigation shows that whenever the unemployment rate increases by 1%, the death rate increases correspondingly by 2%.**

这个句子中有一个that引导的宾语从句，从句做shows的宾语。whenever相当于no matter when, conj.每当；无论何时；随时。

例 I'd like to see you whenever it's convenient.
在你方便的时候我想来看看你。

She gets in a fret whenever we're late.
只要我们一迟到，她就焦虑不安。

increase by 表示"增加多少，以……的幅度增加"，注意介词by的使用。

例 We figured that the output would increase by 5%.
我们盘算了一下，产量将增加百分之五。

Export to Africa has increased by more than 25%.
对非洲的出口增长了25%。

② **All this comes down to one point: work is helpful to health.**

come down to 可归结为

例 The two lovers are living in a kind of dream world; but they'll come down to earth.
这两个相爱的人生活在一种梦幻世界中；但他们终要回到现实中来。

If you come down to the old price, we can place an order of a large quantity.
贵方若能降到老价格，我们就向您大量订货。

be helpful to 有助于……；对……有益

例 Lionel asked me how things were going at work, but I suspect he was just fishing for information that might be helpful to his own company.
莱昂内尔问我工作情况如何，不过我怀疑他只是想探听一些可能对他自己公司有帮助的消息。

③ **Many high achievers who love their careers feel they are most happy when they are working hard.**

这个句子中有一个who引导的定语从句，先行词是achievers，从句是对先行词的解释说明，who在从句中充当主语成分。后面还有一个when引导的时间状语从句。

④ **From the above we can come to the conclusion that the more you work, the happier and healthier you will be.**

From the above 综上所述

例 Things like fashion, movies, literature are evolved from the above.
而像时尚、电影、文学都是从以上进化而来的。

come to the conclusion 作出结论（得出结论）

例 I've known Steve for a year now, but I have reluctantly come to the conclusion that he's a fool.
现在我已认识史蒂夫一年了，可是我却不情愿地得出他是一个傻瓜的结论。

After a few months I came to the conclusion that effective steps would have to be taken if we were to win the competition.
几个月后，我得出结论：如果我们要在竞争中取胜，就必须采取有效的措施。

经典名句 Famous Classics

1. Life is fine and enjoyable, yet you must learn to enjoy your fine life.
人生是美好的，但要学会如何享用美好的生活。

2. Life is but a hard and tortuous journey.
人生即是一段艰难曲折的旅程，人生无坦途。

3. Life is a horse, and either you ride it or it rides you.
人生像一匹马，你不驾驭它，它便驾驭你。

4. Life is like music. It must be composed by ear, feeling and instinct, not by rule.
人生如一首乐曲，要用乐感、感情和直觉去谱写，不能只按乐律行事。

5. There's only one corner of the universe you can be sure of

Hard Work Is Good for Health
努力工作有利健康

improving, and that's your own self.
这个宇宙中只有一个角落你肯定可以改进，那就是你自己。

6. The world is like a mirror: Frown at it and it frowns at you; smile, and it smiles too.
世界犹如一面镜子：朝它皱眉它就朝你皱眉，朝它微笑它也朝你微笑。

7. The greatest test of courage on earth is to bear defeat without losing heart.
世界上对勇气的最大考验是忍受失败而不丧失信心。

8. Only they who fulfill their duties in everyday matters will fulfill them on great occasions.
只有在日常生活中尽责的人才会在重大时刻尽责。

读书笔记

13 Wake up Your Life
激发生活的热情

Years ago, when I started looking for my first job, wise advisers urged, "Barbara, be enthusiastic! Enthusiasm will take you further than any amount of experience."

How right they were. Enthusiastic people can turn a boring drive into an adventure, extra work into opportunity and strangers into friends.

"Nothing great was ever achieved without enthusiasm, " wrote Ralph Waldo Emerson. It is the **paste** that helps you hang in there when the going gets tough. It is the inner voice that **whispers**, "I can do it!" when others shout, "No, you can't."

We are all born with wide-eyed, enthusiastic wonder-as anyone knows who has ever seen an **infant**'s delight at the **jingle** of keys or the **scurrying** of a battle.

It is this childlike wonder that gives enthusiastic people such a youthful air, whatever their age. As poet and author Samuel Ullman once wrote, "Years wrinkles the skin, but to give up enthusiasm wrinkles the soul."

We need to live each moment

多年以前，当我开始寻找我的第一个工作时，我得到明智的建议，"巴巴拉，要热情！热情会比大量的经验带给你更大的成功。"

这话多么正确，热情的人把沉闷的车程变成探险，把加班变成机会，把陌生人变成朋友。

"没有热情就成就不了伟大的事业。"拉尔夫·沃尔多·爱默森写到。当进展变得困难时，就是这种像浆糊一般有黏性的热诚帮助你坚忍下去。当别人喊道"你做不到"时，这个来自内心的声音低语道："你可以的。"

我们从一出生，就睁大眼睛，热情地探索这个世界——我们每个人都见过婴儿在听到钥匙叮当的碰撞声或者看到甲虫快速爬动时那欣喜的样子。

就是这种孩子般的好奇给了热情的人们如此年轻的空气，无论他们多大年龄。就像诗人、作家塞缪尔·厄尔曼曾经写道："年龄给皮肤带来皱纹，但是放弃热情则使灵魂衰老。"

我们需要全心全意，用我

wholeheartedly, with all our senses-finding pleasure in the **fragrance** of a back-yard garden, the crayoned picture of a six-year-old, the **enchanting** beauty of a rainbow. It is such enthusiastic love of life that puts a **sparkle** in our eyes, a lilt in our steps and **smoothes** the wrinkles from our souls.

们所有的感知度过生命中的每一刻——在后院花园里的芳香中，在六岁孩子的蜡笔画中，在美丽的彩虹中寻找快乐。就是这种对生活的热情和爱使我们的眼睛变得闪亮。正是这种生活中充满激情的爱，才会使我们的双眼闪烁着光芒，使我们脚步轻松欢快，抚平我们心灵中的那些皱纹。

单词解析 Word Analysis

paste [peɪst] *n.* 面团；浆糊；糊状物；糊

例 We used paste to attach our designs to the poster.
我们用浆糊把我们设计的图案贴在招贴牌上。

whisper ['wɪspər] *vi.* 低声说；窃窃私语；飒飒地响 *vt.* 耳语；私语

例 The children were whispering in the corner.
孩子们正在角落里低声耳语。

infant ['ɪnfənt] *n.* 婴儿；幼儿

例 My sister's infant is very lovely.
我姐姐的小婴儿非常可爱。

jingle ['dʒɪŋgl] *n.* 叮当声；广告歌

例 The key fell on the ground with a jingle.
钥匙叮当落地。

scurrying ['skɜːri] *n.* 快跑声；疾走

例 I heard a scurry of footsteps.
我听到一阵匆忙奔跑的脚步声。

wholeheartedly [ˌhəʊlˈhɑːtɪdli] *adv.* 尽力；全心全意地

例 We will support you wholeheartedly.
我们将会全心全意地支持您。

fragrance [ˈfreɪɡrəns] *n.* 香味

例 The flowers send forth special fragrance.
这些花散发出特别的香味。

enchanting [ɪnˈtʃæntɪŋ] *adj.* 迷人的

例 If you do not mind my saying so, your smile is quite enchanting.
如果您不介意我这么说的话，您的微笑很迷人。

sparkle [ˈspɑːkl] *n.* 闪耀；火花

例 There was a sparkle of excitement in her eyes.
她眼里闪耀着激动的光芒。

smooth [smuːð] *v.* 使光滑；消除；安慰；理顺（羽毛）

例 No matter how hard she tried, she was unable to smooth over their differences.
不管她怎么努力，也未能消除他们之间的分歧。

语法知识点 Grammar Points

① It is the paste that helps you hang in there when the going gets tough.

这个句子中，it is...that...是强调句结构，去掉之后句子仍然完整。后面还有一个when引导的时间状语从句。

hang in 坚持

例 No matter how long it takes, just hang in there.
不管这事花多长时间，都要坚持下去。

A giant photograph of the actor hang in the foyer of the theatre.
那位演员的巨幅照片挂在剧场的休息室里。

Wake up Your Life
激发生活的热情

② **We are all born with wide-eyed, enthusiastic wonder-as anyone knows who has ever seen an infant's delight at the jingle of keys or the scurrying of a battle.**

这个句子中有一个who引导的定语从句，先行词是anyone，who在从句中充当主语成分。

be born with 生而具有

例 Not everyone was born with such endowments as you.
并非所有的人生来都像你这样有天赋。
He was born with a slight deformity of the feet which made him limp.
他的脚稍有先天畸形，走起路来一瘸一拐。

经典名句 Famous Classics

1. The shortest way to do many things is to do only one thing at a time.
做许多事情的捷径就是一次只做一件事。

2. Our virtues are most frequently but vices in disguise.
我们所谓的美德往往只是被掩盖的丑恶。

3. Life would be too smooth if it had no rubs in it.
生活若无波折险阻，就会过于平淡无奇。

4. If we hate a person, we hate something in our image of him that lies within ourselves. What is not within ourselves doesn't upset us.
当我们憎恨某人时，我们恨的是这个人身上与自己相同的一部分，我们自己没有的部分也不会让我们讨厌。

5. Roses have thorns, and silver fountains mud; Clouds and eclipses stain both moon and sun, and loathsome canker lives in sweetest bud. All men make faults.
玫瑰总是带着尖刺，银色的泉水下总有淤泥。云与蚀使日月黯淡无光，最鲜嫩的花苞也会腐烂，人们也都会犯下错误。

6. All things in their being are good for something.
天生我才必有用。

7. The road to health for everyone is through moderation, harmony, and a sound mind in a sound body.
   对每个人来说,保持健康的途径都是节制饮食,保持和谐,并且拥有美好的心灵。

8. Self-distrust is the cause of most of our failures.
   我们绝大多数的失败都是因为缺乏自信之故。

读书笔记

14 On Idleness
论懒惰

There are some that **profess** Idleness in its full dignity, who call themselves the Idle, who **boast** that they do nothing, and thank their stars that they have nothing to do; who sleep every night till they can sleep no longer, and rise only that exercise may enable them to sleep again; who **prolong** the **reign** of darkness by double curtains, and never see the sun but to tell him how they hate his **beams**; whose whole **labor** is to vary the **postures** of **indulgence**, and whose day differs from their night but as a couch or chair differs from a bed.

These are the true and open votaries of Idleness, for whom she weaves the **garlands** of **poppies**, and into whose cup she pours the waters of **oblivion**; who exist in a state of **unruffled** stupidity, forgetting and forgotten; who have long ceased to live, and at whose death the survivors can only say, that they have ceased to breathe.

But idleness **predominates** in many lives where it is not suspected; for being a vice which **terminates** in itself, it may be enjoyed without injury to others; and

有一些人声称懒惰也有它充分的尊严，这些人叫自己懒人，他们吹嘘自己什么都不做，也感谢上帝他们什么都不用做；他们每天都睡到自然醒，然后做一些运动，只有那样他们才能再次入睡；他们用两层窗帘延长黑暗的时间，从来不见太阳却告诉太阳他们讨厌它的光；他们所做的一切就是变换一下沉昏的姿态，对于他们来说，白天与黑夜的区别只不过相当于从沙发或椅子上挪到床上。

这些人是懒散女神真正公开的崇拜者，女神为他们佩戴罂粟花环，在他们的杯子里倾倒忘却之水；他们浑浑噩噩地活着，度日如年，忘却了他人也被他人所遗忘；他们早就停止了生活，他们死去时，活着的人也只会说他们不再呼吸。

懒散主宰了许多人的生活，而不为人所知；作为一种恶习，在不伤害他人的情况下被享受着；因而人们对懒散不像对危及他人财产的诈骗和自然而然地在从他人的自卑中寻

it is therefore not watched like fraud, which endangers property, or like pride, which naturally seeks it **gratifications** in another's **inferiority**. Idleness is a silent and peaceful quality that neither raises envy by **ostentation**, nor hatred by opposition; and therefore nobody is busy to censure or detest it.

There are others to whom Idleness **dictates** another expedient, by which life may be passed unprofitably away without the **tediousness** of many vacant hours. The art is, to fill the day with petty business, to have always something in hand which may raise curiosity, but not **solicitude**, and keep the mind in a state of action, but not of labor.

No man is so much open to conviction as the idler, but there is none on whom it operates so little. What will be the effect of this paper I know: perhaps he will read it and laugh, and light the fire in his **furnace**; but my hope is that he will quit his **trifles**, and betake himself to **rational** and useful diligence.

求满足的骄傲那样保持警惕。懒散不显山不露水，既不会由于炫耀而招致嫉妒，也不会因为对抗而遭人憎恨。正因为如此，没有人指责它，憎恶它。

对于其他一些人来说，懒散还有另一种表现形式，时光纵然白白流逝，而他们并没有因为许多小时没有做什么而感到无聊乏味。其办法就是一天到晚忙于琐事，手边总有事或许会激起好奇心，却不会让他们牵肠挂肚；大脑总是动个不停，却不会让他们劳神伤思。

没有人愿意承认自己懒，但也几乎没人不受其影响。我不知道这篇文章将会产生什么影响：也许一个人读过之后，哈哈大笑，点燃炉火；但是我希望他能放下琐事，把自己投入到理性的、有用的勤奋工作当中。

单词解析 Word Analysis

profess [prə'fes] v. 声称；冒称；以……为业；正式接受入教；表明信仰

例 They have become what they profess to scorn.
他们成了自己曾声称看不起的那种人。

On Idleness 论懒惰 14

boast [boʊst] *v.* 自夸；吹牛；以……为荣
例 Nobody should boast of his learning.
谁也不应当夸耀自己的学识。

prolong [prəˈlɔːŋ] *vt.* 延长；拖延
例 How can we endeavor to prolong the brevity of human life?
我们怎样才能延长短促的人生？

reign [reɪn] *n.* 君主统治；在位期
例 People will remember the tyrannies of his reign.
人们不会忘记他统治时期的暴行。

beam [biːm] *n.* 桁条；光线；（光线的）束；（横）梁
例 Hold the flashlight so that the beam shines straight down on a sheet of white paper.
手握电筒让光线直射在一张白纸上。

labor [ˈleɪbər] *n.* 工人；劳工；工作；分娩；劳力
例 The country is short of skilled labor.
这个国家缺乏熟练工人。

posture [ˈpɑːstʃər] *n.* 姿势；态度；情形
例 Only humans have a natural upright posture.
只有人类才有自然直立的姿势。

indulgence [ɪnˈdʌldʒəns] *n.* 沉溺；放纵；嗜好
例 I must ask the readers' kind indulgence for any inaccuracies and omissions that may possibly occur.
我必须请求读者原谅可能出现的错误和疏漏。

garland [ˈɡɑːrlənd] *n.* 花环
例 I wove a garland of flowers.
我编了一个花环。

poppy [ˈpɑːpi] *n.* 罂粟；鸦片；芙蓉红
例 The Queen laid a poppy wreath at the war memorial.
女王向阵亡将士纪念碑献了花圈。

oblivion [əˈblɪvɪən] *n.* 遗忘；忘却

例 Many ancient cities are buried in oblivion.
许多古城都已被遗忘了。

unruffled [ʌnˈrʌfld] *adj.* 平静的；镇定的；沉着的；无波浪的

例 He remained unruffled by the charges.
他受到这些指控仍处之泰然。

predominate [prɪˈdɑːmɪneɪt] *v.* 占优势；支配

例 Pine trees predominate the woods here.
这儿的树林中最多的是松树。

terminate [ˈtɜːmɪneɪt] *v.* 结束；终止；满期；达到终点

例 The mission was terminated due to his absence.
由于他的缺席，任务被终止了。

gratification [ˌɡrætɪfɪˈkeɪʃn] *n.* 满足；喜悦

例 Again Hist experienced the profound gratification when he heard the language of praise spoken by those he loved.
听了所爱的人说出这番赞扬的话，希斯特又一次感到由衷的喜悦。

inferiority [ɪnˌfɪriˈɔːrəti] *n.* 自卑；低劣

例 Failure induces a total sense of inferiority.
失败使人产生自卑。

ostentation [ˌɑːstenˈteɪʃn] *n.* 卖弄；虚饰；炫耀

例 The statue had beauty without ostentation.
那座雕像有一种不浮夸的美。

dictate [ˈdɪkteɪt] *v.* 口授；规定；决定，影响

例 You can't dictate to people how they should live.
你不能强行规定人们应该怎样生活。

tediousness [ˈtiːdiəsnəs] *n.* 乏味

例 The clock dragged away the minutes teasing her with the tediousness of the day.
钟摆一分分地过去，好像在嘲弄她乏味的一天。

On Idleness 论懒惰

solicitude [sə'lɪsɪtuːd] *n.* 关心；挂念；焦虑
例 His future is my greatest solicitude.
他的前途是我最关心的问题。

furnace ['fɜːrnɪs] *n.* 炉子；熔炉；闷热地带；严峻考验
例 The metal glowed in the furnace.
金属在熔炉里发出灼热的光。

trifle ['traɪfl] *n.* 琐事；少量
例 They had an altercation about a trifle.
他们为一点小事争吵起来。

rational ['ræʃnəl] *adj.* 合理的；理性的；能推理的
例 Your choice was perfectly rational under the circumstances.
在那种情况下，你的选择是相当合理的。

语法知识点 Grammar Points

① **But idleness predominates in many lives where it is not suspected; for being a vice which terminates in it, it may be enjoyed without injury to others; and it therefore not watched like fraud, which endangers property, or like pride, which naturally seeks it gratifications in another's inferiority.**

这个句子是一个复杂的复合句。首先是一个where引导的定语从句，先行词是many lives。后面是一个which引导的定语从句，和两个which引导的非限制性定语从句。

without injury 无损伤
例 Wash the speck out without injury to your eyes.
把微粒洗出来，但不能损伤眼睛。
He escaped from the train wreck without injury.
他在这次火车事故中没有受伤。
The owner escaped the incident without injury.
车主逃脱事件没有受伤。

② **Idleness is a silent and peaceful quality that neither raises envy by ostentation, nor hatred by opposition; and therefore nobody is busy to censure or detest it.**

这个句子中有一个that引导的定语从句，先行词是a silent and peaceful quality，that在从句中充当主语。

Neither...nor... 既不……也不……

例 He spared neither efforts nor money.
他既不辞辛劳也不惜费用。

It is neither hot nor cold in winter here.
这里冬天既不热也不冷。

He has neither prepared his lesson nor gone to bed.
他没有准备功课也没有睡觉。

③ **No man is so much open to conviction as the idler, but there is none on whom it operates so little.**

not so much...as... 与其说是……不如说是……。so much as 甚至；几乎

例 I lay down not so much to sleep as to think.
我躺下来与其说是要睡觉，倒不如说是要思考。

He is not so much a player as a coach.
与其说他是个队员，不如说他是个教练。

It is not the boy that talks so much as the girl.
这个男孩并不像那个女孩说那样多的话。

It is not his parents that influence him so much as his teachers.
他的父母并不像他的老师对他那样有影响。

经典名句 Famous Classics

1. He that can have patience, can have what he will.
唯坚韧者始能遂其志。

2. Egotism is the anesthetic that dulls the pain of stupidity.
自大是一种麻醉药，让人察觉不到自己的愚蠢。

3. Difficult circumstances serve as a textbook of life for people.
   困难坎坷是人们的生活教科书。

4. He who is in love with himself has at least this advantage —he won't encounter many rivals.
   自恋的好处是不会有太多情敌。

5. Those who turn back never reach the summit.
   回头的人永远到不了最高峰！

6. We can always make ourselves liked provided we are likable, but we cannot always make ourselves esteemed, no matter what our merits are.
   可爱的人总会被人喜欢；但无论是品德多么高尚的人，都不总是能受人尊敬。

7. The talent of success is nothing more than doing well whatever you do without a thought of time.
   成功之路无他，唯全力投入工作，而不稍存沽名钓誉之心。

8. Men have to do some awfully mean things to keep up their respectability.
   人们不得不做出一些非常恶劣的事情来维护自己的名望。

9. Do not, for one repulse, forgo the purpose that you resolved to effort.
   不要只因一次挫败，就放弃你原来决心想达到的目的。

读书笔记

15 Thoughts for a New Year
新年沉思

Most of us look away when we pass strangers. It is the **exceptional** person who stops to help the woman **maneuvering** her kids and **groceries** up the staircase. We rarely give up in line or on the subway or bus. Locked into our automobiles, we prefer **gridlock** to giving way.

These daily **encounters**, when they are angry or alien, **diminish** our lives. When they are pleasant, we feel **buoyed**. Yet when we sit at home and make resolutions, we think about what we can accomplish in private spaces: home, work. Too many have given up the belief that they control the shared, the public world.

As individuals we can change the **contour** of a day, the mood of a moment, the way people feel. The **demolition** and **reconstruction** of public life is the result of personal decisions made every day: the decision to give up a seat on the bus; the decision to be patient or pleasant against all odds; the decision to let that **jerk** take a left-hand turn from a right-hand lane without rolling down the window and

当我们与陌生人擦肩而过时，多数人往往把目光移开。要是有人停下来帮妇女哄她的小孩和帮她把食品搬上楼梯，反而会被人看成另类。无论是排队还是乘地铁或公共汽车，我们很少让位给他人。坐在自己的汽车里，我们宁愿堵塞交通也不愿让路。

这些日常接触，要是气冲冲的或是使人反感的，那便会减少我们生活的乐趣，要是它们令人愉快，那便会使我们精神振奋。然而，当我们坐在家里做出各种决定的时候，我们考虑的仅是在个人天地——家庭和工作里可以实现的目标。太多的人已经放弃了他们也管理着共享的、公共的世界这一信念。

作为众人的一员，我们可以改变一天的面貌、一时的情绪，以及人们对某件事的感觉。公共生活的毁坏和重建是人们每日所做的种种个人决定的综合结果。这些决定包括：公共汽车上让座，面对逆境而能容忍或具有乐观精神；让那

calling him a jerk.

It's the resolution to be a civil, social creature. This may be a peak period for the battle against the spread of a **waistline** and creeping **cholesterol**. But it is also within our will power to fight the spread of **urban** rudeness and creeping hostility. Civility doesn't stop nuclear **holocaust** and doesn't put a roof over the head of the homeless. But it makes a difference in the shape of a community, as surely as lifting weights can make a difference in the shape of a human **torso**.

这是做一个文明的、社会的人的决定。今天也许是人们为减少腰围和降低胆固醇而斗争的高峰期。然而，反对城市野蛮行为和人际敌对态度的蔓延，也是我们只要愿做就能做到的事。有礼貌不能制止核战争，也不能为无家可归者提供栖身之所，但它的确能改变一个社会群体的面貌，犹如举重定能改变一个人的体形一样。

单词解析 Word Analysis

exceptional [ɪkˈsepʃnl] *adj.* 异常的；例外的；特别的；杰出的
- Our circumstances have been rather exceptional.
  我们的情况相当特别。

maneuver [məˈnuːvər] *vt.* 巧妙地操纵；使演习；调遣 *vi.* 演习；调遣；用计策
- They have had to maneuver the ship to avoid unforeseen shoals and shallows.
  他们必须设法避开无法预见的暗礁和浅滩。

grocery [ˈɡroʊsəri] *n.* 杂货店
- Her mother began to operate a small grocery.
  她母亲开始经营一家小杂货店。

gridlock [ˈɡrɪdlɑːk] *n.* 极端严重的全面交通堵塞（无车能动）；僵局
- But he is acknowledging continued partisan gridlock in Congress.
  但他承认在国会党派僵局仍然存在。

encounter [ɪnˈkaʊntər] *n.* 意外的相见；邂逅；遭遇
例 A fortunate encounter brought us together.
一次幸运的邂逅使我们相识。

diminish [dɪˈmɪnɪʃ] *vt.* 减少；减损；贬低 *vi.* 变少；逐渐变细
例 We should try to diminish the cost of production.
我们应尽力减少生产成本。

buoy [bɔɪ] *v.* 使浮起；支持；鼓励；用浮标指示 *n.* 浮标；浮筒；救生圈；救生衣
例 At turns, everybody bunches up as close to the buoy as they can.
在转弯的地方，大家都尽可能往浮标的地方挤。

contour [ˈkɑːntʊr] *n.* 周线；轮廓；等高线；概要；电路
例 The contour of that mountain looks like a dragon.
那座大山的轮廓看上去像一条龙。

demolition [ˌdeməˈlɪʃn] *n.* 破坏；毁坏
例 Demolition runs in the family.
这个家族就是擅长搞破坏。

reconstruction [ˌriːkənˈstrʌkʃn] *n.* 复兴；改造；再建
例 The World Bank was created with European reconstruction in mind.
世界银行是考虑到为欧洲复兴而创建的。

jerk [dʒɜːrk] *n.* 猛拉；急动；笨蛋
例 The knife was stuck, but she pulled it out with a jerk.
那把刀子被卡住了，她猛地一拔，把它拔了出来。

waistline [ˈweɪstlaɪn] *n.* 腰围；腰身部分
例 This is a dress with a high waistline.
这条裙子腰线很高。

cholesterol [kəˈlestərɔːl] *n.* 胆固醇
例 This cooking oil is low in cholesterol.

Thoughts for a New Year
新年沉思

这种烹调油胆固醇含量低。

urban ['ɜːrbən] *adj.* 城市的；都市的

例 In some developing countries more and more people are migrating to urban areas.
在某些发展中的国家，越来越多的人向市区迁移。

holocaust ['hɑːləkɔːst] *n.* 大屠杀；浩劫；燔祭

例 He was a descendent of Holocaust survivors.
他是大屠杀幸存者的后代。

torso ['tɔːrsoʊ] *n.* 躯干；残缺的东西；人体的躯干雕塑像

例 Kicking involves the torso as well as the legs and feet.
踢腿包括躯干、腿和脚的动作。

语法知识点 Grammar Points

① **It is the exceptional person who stops to help the woman maneuvering her kids and groceries up the staircase. We rarely give up in line or on the subway or bus.**

这个句子中用了强调句结构it is...who...，去掉后句子结构仍然完整。

例 It is only shallow people who judge by appearances.
只有浅薄的人才会以貌取人。

give up *v.* 放弃；抛弃；戒除；交出

例 You ought to give up smoking; I gave it up last year.
你应该戒烟，我去年就戒掉了。

② **The demolition and reconstruction of public life is the result of personal decisions made every day: the decision to give up a seat on the bus; the decision to be patient or pleasant against all odds; the decision to let that jerk take a left - hand turn from a right - hand lane without rolling down the window and calling him a jerk.**

这个句子很长，前面是主句，后面是解释说明，是几个并列短语。
the result of ……的结果

例 He is indifferent to the result of the exam.
他对考试结果漠不关心。
What was the result of your deliberation?
你仔细考虑后结果如何？
The treaty was the result of long negotiation.
这项条约是长时间谈判的结果。

against all odds 不顾一切

例 Against all odds she achieved her dream.
她冲破重重困难，实现了自己的梦想。
He was admitted to graduate school against all odds.
不顾一切反对意见，他被录取为研究生。
That you come back to me is against all odds.
让你回到我身边必有重重困难。
He survived the cancer against all odds.
他勇敢地与癌症做斗争活了下来。

roll down 滚下

例 As the rock rolled down the mountainside, it gathered momentum.
石头滚下山时，它的动量增加。
As his voice rose, the tears began to roll down her cheeks.
随着他的嗓音提高，她的眼泪开始簌簌地直往下流。

③ **Civility doesn't stop nuclear holocaust and doesn't put a roof over the head of the homeless.**

put a roof over the head of 为……提供栖身之所，安顿下来

例 Let's put a roof over our head.
咱们找个地方安顿吧。
My new house is not a palace, but at least it means I have a roof over my head.
我的新居不是一座宫殿，但至少我有了自己的栖身之处。

④ **But it makes a difference in the shape of a community, as surely as lifting weights can make a difference in the shape of a human torso.**

Thoughts for a New Year 新年沉思 15

make a difference 有影响；起（重要）作用

- One honest man can make a difference.
  有一个老实人就可以大变样。
- I will make a difference in this world!
  我要让这世界有所不同！

in the shape of 以……形状；通过……方式

- I'll just rough in the shape of the head and you can paint the sky round it.
  我把头形勾勒出来，你可以在头四周画上天空。
- I received a nasty surprise in the shape of a letter from the taxman.
  我收到税务局的来信，把我吓得六神无主。
- The garden is in the shape of a square.
  这花园是方形的。

as surely as / as sure as 毫无疑问

- Whenever I'm late, as sure as fate I meet the boss on the stairs.
  像命中注定的，每次迟到我都在楼梯上碰到老板。
- As surely as egg is egg, it will rain tomorrow.
  明天肯定会下雨。

lift weights 举重

- My muscles are sore from lifting weights.
  我的肌肉因为举重而感到酸痛。
- I lift weights every day in the gym.
  我每天都到体育馆练习举杠铃。

经典名句 Famous Classics

1. Bad times make a good man.
   艰难困苦出能人。

2. It's not that I'm afraid to die. I just don't want to be there when it happens.
   我不是害怕死亡，我只是不想到时候在场。

3. There is no royal road to learning.
   求知无坦途。

4. Any man's death diminishes me, because I am involved in Mankind; And therefore never send to know for whom the bell tolls; it tolls for thee.
   每个人的死去都使我更加衰弱，因为我是人类中的一分子；所以不要派人去问丧钟为谁而鸣；丧钟为你而鸣。

5. Doubt is the key to knowledge.
   怀疑是知识的钥匙。

6. Sharp tools make good work.
   工欲善其事，必先利其器。

7. Wasting time is robbing oneself.
   浪费时间就是掠夺自己。

8. There is no garden without its weeds.
   没有不长杂草的花园。

读书笔记

16 What's Your Spiritual IQ?
什么是你的精神智商?

Spiritual intelligence is the capacity to sense, understand and tap into the highest part of ourselves, of others and of the world around us. This source of inner **serenity** may be our best defense against the **hassles** that **barrage** us every day.

While we're all born with SQ, most of us aren't even aware that we have it. Fortunately, you don't have to sign up for classes to learn how to **enhance** your SQ. Here are some simple steps that can lead you to this new level of understanding:

Sit Quietly. The process of cultivating spiritual intelligence begins in **solitude** and silence. Most spiritual traditions involve an inner wisdom. To tune into its whisper, you have to turn down the volume in your busy, noisy, complicated life and force yourself to do nothing at all. Start small by creating islands of silence in your day. In the car, instead of reaching for the radio **dial**, use the time to reflect. At work, shut the door to your office between meetings, take a few deep breaths and let them out very, very slowly. **Savor** the **stillness** in

精神智商是一种能力，可以感受、理解并触及最深的自我、他人及我们周遭的世界。这种内心深处的宁静可能是我们抵御日常困扰的最佳能力。

虽然我们生来就有精神智商，但大多数人并没有意识到它的存在。幸运的是，你不必报名去学习如何加强你的精神智商。以下几个简单的方法就可帮你达到理解的新境界：

静坐培养。精神智商可从独处和静默开始。精神上的信仰大多需要心灵的智慧。要听到心灵的细语就要放慢节奏，使纷繁嘈杂的生活平静下来，迫使自己放下一切事务。逐渐为每一天创造一段安静的时间。在开车时，用一些时间思考，而不是打开收音机。在工作时，不妨利用会议间歇关上办公室的门，深吸几口气，然后缓缓地呼出。在家里，孩子上床后，独自细细地品味一下家里的宁静。

户外活动。对于许多人来说，大自然能给予他们精神上的自由，使他们对日常生活中烦心

your home after the kids are finally in bed.

Step Outside. For many people, nature sets their spirit free. It puts the hassles of daily living into perspective.

Go outside to watch a beautiful sunset. If you're walking the dog, take the time to admire an **azalea** bush in bloom. Follow the flight of a bird; watch clouds **float** overhead. Gaze into the night sky and think of the stars as holes in the darkness letting heaven shine through.

Find An Activity You Enjoy. It's important to find a hobby that helps you tune in to your spirit. Garden, walk or jog, arrange flowers, listen to music that touches your soul.

Ask Questions Of Yourself. Some people use their **contemplative** time to focus on a line of Scripture. Others ask open-ended questions, such as "What am I feeling? What are my choices? Where am I heading?" But don't expect an answer to arrive via some supernatural form of e-mail. "**Rarely** do I get an immediate answer to my questions," says Reverend Joan Carter, a Presbyterian minister in Sausalito, California. "But later that day I suddenly find myself thinking about a problem from a perspective I never considered before."

的事能用不同的角度去看待。

出去观看美丽的日出。如果出门遛狗，可以留意一下路边盛开的杜鹃花丛；可以仰望飞翔的小鸟；观赏空中的浮云。凝视夜空，可以设想群星不过是黑幕上的点点小洞，让天堂之光透射进来。

找到一种自己喜爱的活动，培养一种爱好对修身养性十分重要。例如：园艺、散步或慢跑、插花、倾听触动心灵的音乐。

向自己提问。一些人在沉思中思考圣经中的语句。另一些人问自己一些随意的问题，如"我现在感觉怎样？我的选择是什么？我现在去往何处？"但是不要期望以超自然的电子邮件方式得到答案。加利福尼亚州，索萨利托的长老会牧师雷弗伦德·琼·卡特说："对自问问题，很少能立刻得到答案，但晚些时候，我会突然从不曾考虑到的另一个角度去思考这个问题。"

相信自己的心灵。大多数人觉察危险是凭直觉。精神智商却常常引导我们去采取某种可以使结局更好的行动，而不是逃避。

What's Your Spiritual IQ?
什么是你的精神智商？ 16

Trust Your Spirit. While most of us rely on gut feelings to **alert** us to danger, spiritual intelligence usually **nudges** us, not away from, but toward some action that will lead to a greater good.

单词解析 Word Analysis

serenity [sə'renəti] *n.* 宁静；沉着

例 I enjoyed the serenity and the peacefulness when I was in the church.
当我身处大教堂时感到平和与宁静。

hassle ['hæsl] *n.* 困难；争吵；麻烦

例 Traveling during peak season can be a hassle.
在旺季旅行可能是个麻烦。

barrage [bə'rɑːʒ] *vt.* 以密集火力进攻

例 Make your opponents spin and crash as you bombard them with a barrage of weapons.
向你的竞争对手们进行重火力袭击，让他们晕头转向并一一被摧毁。

enhance [ɪn'hæns] *vt.* 提高；增加；加强

例 He made many efforts to enhance his reputation.
他做了许多努力来提高他的声誉。

solitude ['sɑːlətuːd] *n.* 孤独；独居；荒僻之地；幽静的地方

例 He passed twenty-four years in solitude.
他在孤独中度过了二十四年。

dial ['daɪəl] *n.* 拨号盘；刻度盘；日晷；钟面

例 The phone number is on the dial.
号码就在拨号盘上。

savor ['seɪvə] *vt.* 调味；品尝；欣赏

例 So next time you savor a new candy or potato chip, thank the flavorists.
所以下回你品尝新口味的糖果或土豆片时，要特别感谢这些调味学家。

stillness ['stɪlnəs] *n.* 静止；沉静

例 At twilight, the stillness was broken by the sound of hooves, clattering on the paved courtyard.
在一个黄昏，沉静被庭院上一阵清脆的马蹄声所打破。

azalea [əˈzeɪliə] *n.* 杜鹃花

例 The azalea was at its brightest.
杜鹃花开得正盛。

float [fləʊt] *v.* 漂浮；浮现；飘动；提出

例 These plants float on the surface of the water.
这些植物漂浮在水面上。

contemplative [kənˈtemplətɪv] *adj.* 沉思的；爱默想的；冥想的

例 The film's pacing is slow and its mood is contemplative.
电影的节奏缓慢，而气氛令人沉思。

rarely ['reəli] *adv.* 很少；难得

例 She rarely went anywhere except to her office.
她除了去办公室以外，很少去别的地方。

alert [əˈlɜːrt] *vt.* 使意识到；警惕

例 I must alert him to the need to solve the problem.
我必须使他认识到解决这问题的必要性。

nudge [nʌdʒ] *vt.* 轻推；轻触；推进

例 I nudged her and pointed to the man across the street.
我用肘碰了她一下并指了指街对面的那个男的。

What's Your Spiritual IQ? 什么是你的精神智商?

语法知识点 Grammar Points

① **This source of inner serenity may be our best defense against the hassles that barrage us every day.**

这个句子中有一个that引导的定语从句，先行词是the hassles，that在从句中充当主语成分。

defense against 为对付……而设的防御

例 The forest will act as a defense against desert dust.
森林能起防御沙漠灰沙的作用。

A thick coat is a good defense against the cold.
厚外衣能防寒。

Arrogance has no defense against a toady.
傲慢防不了谄媚者。

② **While we're all born with SQ, most of us aren't even aware that we have it. Fortunately, you don't have to sign up for classes to learn how to enhance your SQ.**

这个句子中有一个while引导的让步状语从句，后面有一个that引导宾语从句。

born with 天赋的，生而享有

例 He was born with a itching palm.
他生来就贪得无厌。

Not everyone is born with such endowments as you.
并非所有的人生来都像你这样有天赋。

be aware that vt. 知道；察觉到；意识到

例 I was aware that she was trembling.
我察觉到她在发抖。

He was only dimly aware that it was raining.
他只是模模糊糊地意识到天在下雨。

sign up 签约雇用；报名从军；签字参加

例 Many men sign up for the army because they cannot get ordinary jobs.
由于找不到工作，许多男人都报名参了军。

Lucy decided to sign up for yoga classes.
露西决定报名上瑜伽课。

③ **To tune into its whisper, you have to turn down the volume in your busy, noisy, complicated life and force yourself to do nothing at all.**

这个句子中to do不定式表目的。

tune into 收听；收看

例 Voters always elect the candidate who most tuned into their needs.
选民总是选那些最能体察其疾苦的候选人。

Don't forget to tune into our program tomorrow.
明天别忘了继续收看我们的节目。

turn down 调低；关小；拒绝

例 Turn the heat down or your cake will burn.
把热度调低吧，要不蛋糕就要糊了。

Please turn the radio down a bit.
请把收音机关小点。

The board turns down all approaches on the subject of merger.
董事长拒绝了有关合并事宜的任何协商。

She turned down every offer of help.
别人提出的帮助她都拒绝了。

force sb. to do sth. 强迫某人做某事

例 Circumstances force us to adopt this policy.
形势迫使我们采取这项政策。

No power on earth could force me to do it.
世上没人能强迫我做这事。

nothing at all 一无所有；什么都不是；毫无意义

例 He said nothing at all, but his eyes spoke for him.
他什么也没说，但他眼中流露的神情说明了一切。

I know nothing at all about the recent happenings there.
对那里近来发生的事我一点儿也不知道。

The lodger has decamped with paying nothing at all.
房客没付房租就溜走了。

What's Your Spiritual IQ?
什么是你的精神智商？ 16

经典名句 Famous Classics

1. Nothing begins, and nothing ends, that is not paid with moan; for we are born in other's pain, and perish in our own.
   一切的开始与结束，都以痛苦的呻吟为代价；因为我们在别人的痛苦中出生，在自己的痛苦中死亡。

2. Wealth is the test of a man's character.
   财富是对一个人品格的试金石。

3. Live as long as you may, the first twenty years are the longest half of your life.
   不管你活得多么久，二十岁以前的时光总是你生命的一大半。

4. The best hearts are always the bravest.
   心灵最高尚的人，也总是最勇敢的人。

5. What? Is man only a mistake made by God, or God only a mistake made by man?
   究竟是怎样的呢？是上帝错误地创造了人类，还是人类错误地创造了上帝呢？

6. Courtesy is the inseparable companion of virtue.
   礼貌和美貌是分不开的伴侣。

7. Good is good, but better carries it.
   精益求精，善益求善。

8. Politeness costs nothing and gains everything.
   礼貌不用花一分钱，却能赢得一切。

9. Conceit is the quicksand of success.
   自负是成功的流沙。

10. He that makes a good war makes a good peace.
    正义的战争创造持久的和平。

17 Life Without Failure
人生没有失败

Good evening.

Just moments ago, I spoke with George W. Bush and congratulated him on becoming the 43rd president of the United States and I promised him that I wouldn't call him back this time.

I offered to meet with him as soon as possible so that we can start to heal the divisions of the campaign and the contest through which we just passed.

Almost a century and a half ago, Senator Stephen Douglas told Abraham Lincoln, who had just defeated him for the presidency, "Partisan feeling must yield to patriotism, I'm with you, Mr. President, and God bless you."

Well, in that same spirit I say to President-elect Bush that what remains of partisan rancor must now be put aside and may God bless his **stewardship** of this country.

Neither he nor I **anticipated** this long and difficult road. Certainly neither of us wanted it to happen. Yet it came and now it has ended, resolved, as it must be resolved, through the honored institutions of our democracy.

Over the library of one of our great

晚上好。

我刚与乔治·W.布什通过电话，祝贺他成为美国第43届总统，而且我也向他保证这次我不会再给他回电了。

我提议我们应尽快会面，以便消除在刚刚结束的竞选和辩论中产生的分歧。

一个半世纪以前，参议员史蒂芬·道格拉斯对刚刚打败他成为总统的亚伯拉罕·林肯说："党派之争必须服从爱国主义。我支持你，总统先生，愿上帝保佑你。"

本着同样的精神，我要告诉总统当选人布什，现在我们必须搁置党派之间的积怨，愿上帝保佑他管理好这个国家。

无论是他还是我都没有想到竞选之道路竟是如此漫长而艰辛。当然我们也都不希望这样。但事情还是发生了，而且现在已经结束了，已经正式决定了，它必须通过崇高的民主机制来解决。

在我国一所著名法学院的图书馆里刻着这样一句格言："我们生活在上帝和法律之

Life Without Failure
人生没有失败

law schools is **inscribed** the **motto**, "not under man but under god and law." That's the ruling principle of American freedom, the source of our democratic liberties. I've tried to make it my guide throughout this contest as it has guided America's deliberations of all the complex issues of the past five weeks.

Now the U.S Supreme Court has spoken. Let there be no doubt. While I strongly disagree with the court's decision, I accept it. I accept the **finality** of this outcome which will be **ratified** next Monday in the Electoral College. And tonight, for the sake of our unity as a people and the strength of our democracy, I offer my **concession**.

I also accept my responsibility which I will discharge unconditionally to honor the new president-elect and do everything possible to help him bring Americans together in fulfillment of the great vision that our *Declaration of Independence* defines and that our *Constitution* affirms and defends.

Let me say how grateful I am to all those who supported me and supported the cause for which we have fought. Tipper and I feel a deep gratitude to Joe and Hadassah Liebennan who brought passion and high purpose to our partnership and opened new doors not just for our campaign but for our country.

下，而非君主之下。"这是美国自由的主要原则，也是我们民主自由的源泉。我一直试着在竞选过程中践行这一格言，就像在过去5周里，它也曾指导美国对所有复杂问题的深入思考一样。

现在，美国最高法院已经做出决定。毫无疑问，尽管我不赞同最高法院的判决，但是我会接受它。我接受下周一选举团将会认可的结果。今晚，为了国人的万众一心和民主的力量，我做出让步。

我也会接受，同时无条件地履行我的职责，支持总统当选人，尽一切所能帮助他团结美国人民，实现《独立宣言》所描绘的、《宪法》所肯定和维护的美好前景。

请允许我向所有支持我和我们所奋斗的事业的人们表示衷心的感谢。我和蒂佩尔深深地感谢乔和哈达莎·利伯曼。他们为我们的伙伴关系带来了热情和崇高的目标，不仅为竞选也为我们的国家开辟了新的道路。

这是一场非比寻常的大选。但是，在上帝铺设的这条未知道路上，这个迟迟才被打破的僵局会把我们指向一个全新的共同的立场上，因为在这

This has been an **extraordinary** election. But in one of God's unforeseen paths, this belatedly broken impasse can point us all to a new common ground, for its very closeness can serve to remind us that we are one people with a shared history and a shared destiny.

Indeed, that history gives us many examples of contests as hotly debated, as fiercely fought, with their own challenges to the popular will.

Other disputes have dragged on for weeks before reaching resolution. And each time both the victor and the vanquished have accepted the result peacefully and in the spirit of reconciliation. So let it be with us. I know that many of my supporters are disappointed. I am too. But our disappointment must be overcome by our love of country.

And I say to our fellow members of the world community, let no one see this contest as a sign of American weakness. The strength of American democracy is shown most clearly through the difficulties it can overcome.

Some have expressed concern that the unusual nature of this election might **hamper** the next president in the conduct of his office. I do not believe it needs be so. President-elect Bush **inherits** a nation whose citizens will be

种局面中双方非常接近的竞选结果提醒我们，我们是一个民族，拥有同样的历史和命运。

的确，那段历史给了我们许多竞争的例子，比如说竞争者们带着他们对公众意愿的质疑进行激烈的辩论或者残酷的斗争。

其他的争辩在得到解决前往往要耗上几个星期。但是每一次，胜利者和失败者都会本着和解的精神平静地接受结果。因此，让这些精神与我们同在吧。我知道很多支持我的人都很失望，我也是。但我们必须用我们的爱国之心代替失望。

我要对世界上所有的人说，这次竞选不是美国软弱的体现。通过克服各种困难，美国民主的力量得到了最为清楚的彰显。

有些人担心，这次选举一反常态，可能会影响下一任总统的政策实施。我不认同这种顾虑。新任总统布什所接管的这个国家的每一个公民都随时准备帮助他履行这一伟大的职责。

我本人愿意随时任他差遣，而且我要呼吁所有美国人，尤其是那些曾经和我同一战线的人们，团结起来支持我们的下一任总统。这就是美

Life Without Failure
人生没有失败 17

ready to assist him in the conduct of his large responsibilities.

I personally will be at his disposal and I call on all Americans — I particularly urge all who stood with us to unite being our next president. This is America. Just as we fight hard when the stakes are high, we close ranks and come together when the contest is done.

And while there will be time enough to debate our continuing differences, now is the time to recognize that that which unites us is greater than that which divides us.

国。当困难重重时，我们奋力拼搏；当胜负已成定局时，我们摒弃门户之见，团结一心。

既然将来我们会有足够的时间辩论我们之间依然存在的分歧，此刻我们该认清一点：团结我们的力量比拆散我们的力量更能使我们国家强大。

单词解析 Word Analysis

stewardship ['stju:ədʃɪp] *n.* 管理工作；管事人之职位及职责

例 Under his stewardship, the UN's repute has risen immeasurably.
在他的管理下，联合国的声望得到了极大提升。

anticipate [æn'tɪsɪpeɪt] *vt.* 预期，期望

例 At the time we couldn't have anticipated the result of our campaigning.
当时我们不可能预期到我们活动的结果。

inscribe [ɪn'skraɪb] *vt.* 铭刻

例 Some galleries commemorate donors by inscribing their names on the walls.
一些展览馆把捐赠者的名字刻在墙上以纪念他们。

motto ['mɒtəʊ] *n.* 座右铭；格言；箴言；主题句

例 Our motto is "Plan for the worst and hope for the best".
我们的格言是"做最坏的打算，抱最大的希望"。

finality [faɪ'nælɪtɪ] *n.* 定局；终结；结尾

例 Young children have difficulty grasping the finality of death.
小孩子很难理解死亡的终局性。

ratified ['rætɪfaɪd] *v.* 批准，签认（合约等）(ratify 的过去式和过去分词)

例 After 10 years of negotiation, the Senate ratified *the Strategic Arms Reduction Treaty*.
经过10年协商，参议院已经正式批准了《削减战略武器条约》。

concession [kən'seʃ(ə)n] *n.* 让步

例 Farmers were granted concessions from the government to develop the farms.
农民已获得政府授权开发这些农场。

extraordinary [ɪk'strɔːdnrɪ] *adj.* 非凡的；特别的

例 We've made extraordinary progress as a society in that regard.
我们社会在那方面已经取得了巨大进步。

hamper ['hæmpə] *vt.* 妨碍；束缚

例 The bad weather hampered rescue operations.
恶劣的天气阻碍了救助行动。

inherit [ɪn'herɪt] *vt.* 继承，继任

例 He has no son to inherit his land.
他没有儿子来继承田产。

语法知识点 Grammar Points

① **I offered to meet with him as soon as possible so that we can start to heal the divisions of the campaign and the contest through which we just passed.**

本句中so that引导目的状语从句。目的状语从句是指从句部分是用以补充说明主句中谓语动词发生的目的的状语从句。表示目的状语的从句可以由 that, so that, in order that, lest, for fear that, in case 等词引导；目的状语从句的谓语常含有 may, might, can, could, should, will, would 等情态动词。

Life Without Failure
人生没有失败 17

例 You must speak louder so that /in order that you can be heard by all.
你必须大点声说，以便让别人听清你说的话。

② **Over the library of one of our great law schools is inscribed the motto, "not under man but under god and law."**

这个句子中有一结构not...but...表示"不是……而是……"。

例 Did you hear that clearly? We are fighting our own fear, not death but fear.
你清楚地听到没？我们在与我们自己的恐惧做斗争。不是死亡，而是恐惧。

③ **Let there be no doubt. While I strongly disagree with the court's decision, I accept it.**

本句中while引导让步状语从句。while引导的让步状语从句要放在句首，而且让步的语气比though、although等要弱。

例 While I admit his good points, I can see his shortcomings.
尽管我承认他的优点，我还看到他的缺点。

④ **And tonight, for the sake of our unity as a people and the strength of our democracy, I offer my concession.**

本句中for the sake of词组可以置于句首，也可以置于句中，指"为了"的意思（表示做某事的目的）。

例 Let's assume for the sake of argument that we manage to build a satisfactory database.
为了便于讨论，不妨假定我们成功地建立了一个令人满意的数据库。

经典名句 Famous Classics

1. Time is not possession of public property, with the passage of time, the truth exposed increasingly.
时间是不可占有的公共财产，随着时间的推移，真理愈益显露。

2. What makes life dreary is the want of motive.
没有了目的，生活便郁闷无光。

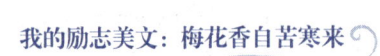

3. Do all the ordinary things well is not ordinary; Do all the simple things well is not simple.
   把一切平凡的事做好就不平凡；把一切简单的事做好就不简单。

4. When we can't afford love, we should never go too close to the window, staring at a happy trance.
   当我们还买不起幸福的时候，我们绝不应该走得离橱窗太近，盯着幸福出神。

5. Life is like a candle, the fire burn and devour the disappearance of the candle in the candle light get eternal moment.
   人生如蜡烛，火的燃烧和吞噬使蜡烛在烛光消失的一瞬间得到永恒。

6. Learning is a bitter coffee, business before pleasure. Only tasted the bitter, can harvest the joy of success.
   学习有如苦咖啡，先苦后甜。只有尝过了苦涩，才会收获成功的喜悦。

7. Man is neither angel, nor beasts; but unfortunately it is to show the angels are shown as the beast.
   人既不是天使，也不是禽兽；但不幸就在于想表现为天使的人却表现为禽兽。

读书笔记

18 The Strenuous Life
勤奋的生活

Gentlemen,

In speaking to you, men of the greatest city of the West, men of the State which gave to the country Lincoln and Grant, men who **preeminently** and distinctly **embody** all that is most American in the American character, I wish to preach not the doctrine of ignoble ease but the **doctrine** of the **strenuous** life; the life of toil and effort; of labor and **strife**; to preach that highest form of success which comes not to the man who desires mere easy peace but to the man who does not shrink from danger, from hardship, of from bitter toil, and who out of these wins the **splendid** ultimate **triumph**.

The timid man, the lazy man, the man who **distrusts** his country, the over civilized man, who has lost the great fighting, masterful virtues, the ignorant man and the man of dull mind, whose soul is **incapable** of feeling the mighty lift that thrills "stem men with empires in their brains"— all these, of course, shrink from seeing the nation undertake its new duties; shrink from seeing us build a navy and army adequate to our needs; shrink from seeing us do our share

先生们：

在向你们——西部最大城市的公民，为国家培育了林肯和格兰特的国家的公民，最能体现美国精神的公民——讲话时，我想谈的不是贪图安逸的人生哲学，而是要向你们宣讲勤奋生活论——过勤奋苦干的生活，过忙碌奋斗的生活。我想说，成功的最高境界不属于满足安逸的人们，而是属于那些在艰难险阻面前从不畏惧终获辉煌的人们。

凡怯懦、懒惰、不相信祖国的人，谨小慎微丧失坚强斗志的"文明过头"的人、混沌无知的人、思想僵化的人、不能像刚毅有抱负的人那样被鼓舞振奋的人——总之，当看到国家有新的责任要承担，当看到祖国正在建立足以满足需要的海陆军，当看到英勇的士兵和水手在美丽的热带岛屿上驱逐西班牙势力，承担起应尽的世界责任，恢复当地秩序——当看到这一切时，所有这些人都退缩了。就是这样一些人，他们害怕过勤奋的生活，害怕过真正值得过的国民的生活。

of the world's work by bringing order out of chaos in the great, fair tropic islands from which the valor of our soldiers and sailors has driven the Spanish flag. These are the men who fear the strenuous life, who fear the only national life which is really worth leading. They believe in that **cloistered** life which saps the hardy **virtues** in a nation, as it saps them in the individual; or else they are wedded to that base spirit of gain and greed which recognizes in **commercialism** the be-all and end-all of national life, instead of realizing that, though an indispensable element, it is after all but one of the many elements that go to make up true national greatness. No country can long endure if its foundations are not laid deep in the material **prosperity** which comes from hard unsparing effort in the fields of industrial activity; but neither was any nation ever yet truly great if it relied upon material prosperity alone. All honor must be paid to the architects of our material prosperity; to the great captains of industry who have built our factories and our railroads; to the strong men who toil for wealth with brain or hand; for great is the debt of the nation to these and their kind. But our debt is yet greater to the men whose highest type is to be found in a statesman like Lincoln, a soldier like Grant. They showed by

他们相信与世隔绝的生活，任由这种生活在侵蚀他们个人吃苦耐劳品德的同时，也侵蚀了一个民族的吃苦耐劳精神。若不然，他们就沉迷于唯利是图、贪得无厌的卑污泥潭而不能自拔，认为国家应一切以商业利益为根本。但他们却不明白，商业利益固然是不可或缺的因素，然而毕竟只是造就真正伟大国家的许多因素之一。诚然，如果一个国家不是深深扎根于通过工业活动领域的艰苦努力所带来的繁荣的物质基础之中，那么这个国家也不可能长久地生存下去。但是，如果仅仅依赖于物质财富，任何国家也永远不会成为真正伟大的国家。我们应该向那些创造了物质财富的人们致敬，向那些创建了工厂和铁路的实业巨头们致敬，向那些用勤劳和智慧换取财富的强者们致敬；国家很感激他们以及和他们一样的人。但是，我们更感激另外一些人，他们的最佳楷模就是林肯那样的政治家和格兰特那样的军人。他们的生活轨迹表明，他们清楚工作和斗争的法则，他们含辛茹苦，使自己和依赖他们生活的人们过上了富足的生活，而且他们懂得还有更崇高的责任——对国家和民

The Strenuous Life
勤奋的生活

their lives that they recognized the law of work, the law of strife; they toiled to win a competence for themselves and those dependent upon them; but they recognized that there were yet other and even loftier duties — duties to the nation and duties to the race.

I preach to you, then, my countrymen, that our country calls not for the life of ease, but for the life of strenuous **endeavor**. The twentieth century looms before us big with the fate of many nations. If we stand idly by, if we seek merely swollen, slothful ease, and ignoble peace, if we shrink from the hard contests where men must win at hazard of their lives and at the risk of all they hold dear, then the bolder and stronger peoples will pass us by and will win for themselves the domination of the world. Let us therefore boldly face the life of strife, resolute to do our duty well and manfully; resolute to uphold **righteousness** by deed and by word; resolute to be both honest and brave, to serve high ideals, yet to use practical methods. Above all, let us shrink from no strife, moral or physical, within or without the nation, provided we are certain that the strife is **justified**; for it is only through strife, through hard and dangerous endeavor, that we shall ultimately win the goal of true national greatness.

族的责任。

所以同胞们，我要讲的是，我们的国家要求我们不能好逸恶劳，而只能过刻苦勤奋的生活。迫在眉睫的20世纪将决定许多国家的命运。假如我们只是一味地袖手旁观、贪图享乐、苟且偷安，假如我们面临激烈的竞争考验时不是冒着牺牲个人生命和失去亲人的危险去赢得胜利，而是落荒而逃的话，那么，更勇敢坚强的民族就会超越我们，得以统领世界。因此，让我们勇敢地面对充满斗争考验的生活，下定决心卓越而果断地履行我们的职责；下定决心无论在语言还是行动上都坚持正义；下定决心诚实勇敢地以切实可行的方法为崇高的理想服务。最重要的是，无论是精神还是物质的斗争，无论是国内还是国外的斗争，只要我们确定正义在手，我们就绝不能逃避退缩。因为只有通过斗争，通过艰苦和充满危险的努力，我们才能最终达到目标——成为真正伟大的国家。

单词解析 Word Analysis

preeminently [prɪˈmaɪnəntlɪ] *adv.* 卓越地，杰出地，超群地

例 This is preeminently the time to speak the truth, the whole truth, frankly and boldly.
现在正是坦白、勇敢地说出实话，说出全部实话的最好时刻。

embody [ɪmˈbɒdɪ] *vt.* 表现，象征；包含，收录；使具体化

例 Google tools embody the new ways of working.
谷歌的工具体现了新的工作方式。

doctrine [ˈdɒktrɪn] *n.* 教条，教义；法律原则；声明

例 Augustine found this doctrine subversive and distasteful.
奥古斯丁发现这个教条具有破坏性并令人厌恶。

strenuous [ˈstrenjuəs] *adj.* 费力的，用力的

例 Avoid strenuous exercise the day before so you go into your run with fresh legs.
避免在长跑之前做费力的训练，这样你就可以双腿充满活力地开始了。

strife [straɪf] *n.* 冲突；斗争；争吵

例 Money is a major cause of strife in many marriages.
金钱是造成很多婚姻不和的一个主要原因。

splendid [ˈsplendɪd] *adj.* 壮观的，豪华的

例 In the 19th century its enterprise produced splendid results.
它的进取心在19世纪取得了辉煌的成就。

distrust [dɪsˈtrʌst] *vt.* 不信任；怀疑

例 I don't have any particular reason to distrust them.
我没有任何特别的理由怀疑他们。

incapable [ɪnˈkeɪpəbl] *adj.* 无能力的，不会的；不能的

例 Thus, in the liquidity trap government policy is incapable of stimulating economic growth.
因此，在流动性陷阱中，政府的政策是无法拉动经济增长的。

The Strenuous Life
勤奋的生活 18

cloister ['klɔɪstə(r)] *n.* 修道院的生活；隐居
- A scientist who cloisters himself in his laboratory.
  把自己关在实验室里的科学家。

virtues ['vɜːtʃuːz] *n.* 优点；德行；美德
- Gandhi exemplified the virtues of renunciation, asceticism and restraint.
  甘地体现了克己、禁欲和自我约束的美德。

commercialism [kə'mɜːʃəlɪzəm] *n.* 商业主义，重商主义
- Koons has engrossed himself in a world of commercialism that most modern artists disdain.
  昆斯投身于商界，那是一个大部分现代艺术家所不齿的圈子。

prosperity [prɒ'sperətɪ] *n.* 繁荣；兴旺，昌盛
- The credential's prosperity has made the GMAT a hot "product."
  这项文凭的繁荣使得 GMAT 考试成为一款热门"产品"。

endeavor [en'devə] *n.* 努力，尽力
- The result: innovation is "an active endeavor," the authors write.
  研究的结论是：创新是"积极的努力"，作家写道。

righteousness ['raɪtʃəsnəs] *n.* 正直；正当；正义
- All my righteousness is like filthy rags.
  我所有的正义都像肮脏的破布。

语法知识点 Grammar Points

① **I wish to preach not the doctrine of ignoble ease but the doctrine of the strenuous life.**

这个句子中有一结构 not...but... 表示"不是……而是……"。
- We are fighting our own fear, not death but fear.
  我们在与我们自己的恐惧做斗争。不是死亡，而是恐惧。

② **These are the men who fear the strenuous life, who fear the only national life which is really worth leading.**

本句中第一个who和第二个who均引导主语从句,先行词是the men;which在句中引导非限定性定语从句,先行词the only national life, which 在从句中做主语。句中有一结构, sth. be worth doing表示"某事值得做"。

例 Depending on the fixer-upper, there are many potential improvements that can be worth doing.
依赖于固定器上,有许多潜在的改善可以值得做。

③ **But our debt is yet greater to the men whose highest type is to be found in a statesman like Lincoln, a soldier like Grant.**

本句是由whose引导的定语从句。

④ **Above all, let us shrink from no strife, moral or physical, within or without the nation, provided we are certain that the strife is justified.**

本句中provided (that) 为虚拟句式的用法,由providing/ provided (that)/ on condition that 引导的从句中,根据情况,可用虚拟语气,遵循if条件句谓语动词变换规则。

经典名句 Famous Classics

1. In the stream of life and the world, he will surely like early winter and fall down from the tree of the last piece of leaf, playing alone in the west wind seems to wander aimlessly.
   在人生和世界的激流中,他必然会像初冬从树上飘落下来的最后一片枯叶,在西风残照中孤零零地漫无目的地飘舞。

2. Obstacles and failures, is the most stable to the success of stepping stone, willing to study and use them, they can develop a successful failure.
   障碍与失败,是通往成功最稳靠的踏脚石,肯研究利用它们,便能从失败中培养出成功。

The Strenuous Life
勤奋的生活 18

3. The fate of people thrown into the lowest point, is often the best period of life turning point. If whine about who will miss the opportunity!
命运把人抛入最低谷时，往往是人生转折的最佳期。谁若自怨自艾，必会坐失良机！

4. The surest way to build self-confidence is to do what you fear until you get the experience of success.
征服畏惧建立自信的最快最确实的方法，就是去做你害怕的事，直到你获得成功的经验。

5. Victory is not to defeat the enemy, but to improve oneself. As long as we make progress one percent every day, that is success.
胜利不是战胜敌人，而是提高自己。我们只要每天进步百分之一，那就是成功。

6. To steer the helm of destiny is to struggle. Do not have a trace of fantasy, do not give up a little chance, do not stop working day.
驾驭命运的舵是奋斗，不抱有一丝幻想，不放弃一点机会，不停止一日努力。

7. It is often the temptation of the outside world to make people lose their senses. It is often their desire that makes people exhaust their efforts.
让人失去理智的，常常是外界的诱惑；让人耗尽心力的，往往是自己的欲望。

读书笔记

19 Flying Like a Kite
像风筝一样飞翔

One windy spring day, I observed young people having fun using the wind to fly their kites. **Multicolored** creations of varying shapes and sizes filled the sky like beautiful birds **darting** and dancing. As the strong winds **gusted** against the kites, a string kept them in check.

Instead of blowing away with the wind, they arose against it to achieve great heights. They shook and pulled, but the **restraining** string and the **cumbersome** tail kept them in tow, facing upward and against the wind. As the kites struggled and **trembled** against the string, they seemed to say, "Let me go! Let me go! I want to be free!" They soared beautifully even as they fought the restriction of the string. Finally, one of the kites succeeded in breaking loose. "Free at last, " it seemed to say. "Free to fly with the wind."Yet freedom from restraint simply put it at the mercy of an **unsympathetic breeze**. It **fluttered** ungracefully to the ground and landed in a **tangled** mass of weeds and string against a dead bush. "Free at last", free to lie powerless in the dirt, to be blown

在一个有风的春日，我看到一群年轻人正在迎风放风筝玩乐，各种颜色、各种形状和大小的风筝就好像美丽的鸟儿在空中飞舞。当强风把风筝吹起，牵引线就能够控制它们。

风筝迎风飘向更高的地方，而不是随风而去。它们摇摆着、拉扯着，但牵引线以及笨重的尾巴使它们处于控制之中，并且迎风而上。它们挣扎着、抖动着想要挣脱线的束缚，仿佛在说："放开我！放开我！我想要自由！"即使与牵引线奋力挣扎着，它们依然在美丽地飞翔。终于，一只风筝成功挣脱了。"终于自由了，"它好像在说，"终于可以随风自由飞了！"

然而，脱离束缚的自由使它完全处于无情微风的摆布下。它毫无风度地震颤着向地面坠落，落在一堆乱草之中，线缠绕在一棵死灌木上。"终于自由"使它自由到无力地躺在尘土中，无助地任风沿着地面将其吹走，碰到第一个障碍物便毫无生命地滞留在那

helplessly along the ground, and to lodge lifeless against the first obstruction.

  How much like kites we sometimes are. The Heaven gives us adversity and restrictions, rules to follow from which we can grow and gain strength. Restraint is a necessary counterpart to the winds of opposition. Some of us tug at the rules so hard that we never soar to reach the heights we might have obtained. We keep part of the commandment and never rise high enough to get our tails off the ground.

  Let us each rise to the great heights, recognizing that some of the restraints that we may chafe under are actually the steadying force that helps us ascend and achieve.

里了。

  有时我们真像这风筝啊！上苍赋予我们困境和约束，赋予我们成长和增强实力所要遵从的规则。约束是逆风的必要匹配物。我们中有些人是如此强硬地抵制规则，以至我们从来无法飞到本来能够达到的高度。我们只遵从部分戒律，因此永远不会飞得足够高，使尾巴远离地面。

  让我们每个人都飞到高处吧，并且认识到这一点：有些可能会令我们生气的约束，实际上是帮助我们攀升和实现愿望的平衡力。

单词解析 Word Analysis

multicolored [ˈmʌltɪˌkʌləd] *adj.* 多彩的，彩色的

 Many multicolored tropical fish are kept in the fish tank in his family.
 他家的鱼缸里养了很多五彩缤纷的热带鱼。

dart [dɑːt] *vi.* 使迅速突然移动

 Ingrid darted across the deserted street.
 英格丽德飞奔过空无一人的街道。

gust [gʌst] *n.* 一阵狂风

 A gust of wind drove down the valley.
 一阵狂风刮过山谷。

restraining [rɪ'streɪnɪŋ] *adj.* 抑制的，遏制的，控制的

例 His estranged wife had taken out a restraining order against him.
与他分居的妻子已经申请到了针对他的限制令。

cumbersome ['kʌmbəsəm] *adj.* 笨重的，冗长的

例 Although the machine looks cumbersome, it is actually easy to use.
尽管这台机器看上去很笨重，操作起来却很容易。

tremble ['trembl] *vi.* 发抖；颤动；焦虑；轻轻摇晃

例 His mouth became dry, his eyes widened, and he began to tremble all over.
他嘴唇发干，眼睛圆睁，全身开始颤抖起来。

unsympathetic [ˌʌnˌsɪmpə'θetɪk] *adj.* 不同情的，冷漠无情的

例 Her husband was unsympathetic and she felt she had no one to turn to.
她丈夫并不懂得体恤人，她觉得无人可依靠。

breeze [briːz] *n.* 微风；轻而易举的事

例 And after being an office manager for 20 people, handling my own tiny staff of three is a breeze!
我曾经是管理着20个人的办公室经理，现在领导区区3名员工不费吹灰之力！

flutter ['flʌtə(r)] *vi.* 飘动；鼓翼

例 Her chiffon skirt was fluttering in the night breeze.
她的雪纺裙在晚风中飘动着。

tangled ['tæŋgld] *adj.* 纠缠的；混乱的；杂乱的；紊乱的

例 The wrong shampoo can leave curly hair in a tangled mess.
不合适的洗发水会使卷发纠结成乱糟糟的一团。

语法知识点 *Grammar Points*

① **One windy spring day, I observed young people having fun using the wind to fly their kites.**

本句中observe doing为"看见某人正在做某事",表示当被看见时动作正在进行。

例 The policeman observed the man opening the window.
  警察看到个人正在开窗户。

② **Yet freedom from restraint simply put it at the mercy of an unsympathetic breeze.**

本句中at the mercy of为"受……支配"。

例 Ordinary people are at the mercy of faceless bureaucrats.
  普通人的命运任凭那些平庸刻板的官僚们摆布。

③ **Some of us tug at the rules so hard that we never soar to reach the heights we might have obtained.**

本句中tug at为"(迅猛地)拉,拖,拽"的意思。

例 Though the whole house began to tremble and you felt the old tug at your ankles.
  虽然整个房子开始颤抖,你亦感到那条旧绳索绊住了你的脚踝。

经典名句 *Famous Classics*

1. You have to believe in yourself. That's the secret of success.
   人必须相信自己,这是成功的秘诀。

2. Although the world is full of suffering, it is full also of the overcoming of it.
   虽然世界多苦难,但是苦难总是能战胜的。

3. Everything can be taken from a man but one thing—the freedom to choose his attitude in any given set of circumstances.
   可以拿走人的任何东西,但有一样东西不行,这就是在特定环境下选择自己的生活态度的自由。

4. Life is measured by thought and action, not by time.
衡量生命的尺度是思想和行为,而不是时间。

5. There is no absolute success in the world, only constant progress.
世界上的事没有绝对成功,只有不断的进步。

6. You can lead a man up to the university, but you can't make him think.
你可以把一个人领进大学,但你却无法使他思考。

7. We have no more right to consume happiness without producing it than to consume wealth without producing it.
不创造幸福的人无权享用幸福,正如不创造财富的人无权享用财富一样。

8. No man is happy who does not think himself so.
认为自己不幸福的人就不会幸福。

读书笔记

20 Attitude Is Everything
态度决定一切

Jerry was the kind of guy you love to hate. He was always in a good mood and always had something **positive** to say. When someone would ask him how he was doing, he would reply, "If I were any better, I would be twins!"

He was a **unique** manager because he had several waiters who had followed him around from restaurant to restaurant. The reason the waiters followed Jerry was because of his attitude. He was a natural **motivator**. If an **employee** was having a bad day, Jerry was there telling the employee how to look on the positive side of the **situation**.

Seeing this style really made me curious, so one day I went up to Jerry and asked him, "I don't get it! You can't be a positive person all of the time. How do you do it?"

Jerry replied, "Each morning I wake up and say to myself, 'Jerry, you have two choices today. You can choose to be in a good mood or you can choose to be in a bad mood.' I choose to be in a good mood. Each time something bad happens, I can choose to be a **victim** or I can choose to learn from it. I choose

杰里真是个让人喜欢得不行的家伙。他总是心情愉快、情绪高涨，总能说出积极的话来。每当别人问他一切可好时，他就回答："好得不能再好了！"

他是个与众不同的经理，有好几个服务员都跟着他在不同的餐厅做过。他们跟着杰里是因为他的生活态度。他天生善于激励人，如果哪个雇员不走运了，杰里就会告诉他要往好的一面看。

我对他的生活态度深感好奇，于是有一天我走到杰里跟前问他："我不明白！你不可能事事都顺心，你是怎样做到一直都这么积极乐观的呢？"

杰里回答说："每天早上醒来后我对自己说，'杰里，今天你有两个选择。你可以选择一个好心情，也可以选择一个坏心情。'我选择了好心情；每次有坏事发生时，我可以选择成为受害者，也可以选择从中吸取教训，我选择了从中吸取教训；每当有人向我抱怨时，我可以选择听他们抱怨，

to learn from it. Every time someone comes to me complaining, I can choose to accept their complaining or I can point out the positive side of life. I choose the positive side of life."

"Yeah, right, it's not that easy, " I **protested.**

"Yes, it is, " Jerry said. "Life is all about choices. When you cut away all the **junk**, every situation is a choice. You choose how you react to situations. You choose how people will affect your mood. You choose to be in a good mood or bad mood. The bottom line: It's your choice how you live life."

或者给他们指出生活中积极的一面,我选择了指出生活中积极的一面。"

"对,话是没错,可是做起来可不容易。"我说。

杰里说:"其实也容易,生活就是由很多选择组成的,除去那些不值一提的事情,那么生活中的每件事都是个选择。你可以选择如何回应这些事。你可以选择周围人影响你心情的方式。你可以选择有个好心情或是坏心情。重点是:你可以选择如何来过你的生活。"

单词解析 *Word Analysis*

positive [ˈpɒzətɪv] *adj.* 积极的

例 Be positive about your future and get on with living a normal life.
要对自己的未来充满信心,继续过一种正常的生活。

unique [juˈniːk] *adj.* 独一无二的,独特的;不平常的,特别的

例 Each person's signature is unique.
每个人的签名都是独一无二的。

motivator [ˈməʊtɪveɪtə(r)] *n.* 促进因素,激发因素,激励者

例 It also shows that you are a good communicator and motivator.
同时也表明你是一个好的沟通者和激励者。

employee [ɪmˈplɔɪiː] *n.* 雇工,雇员,职工

例 He is an employee of Fuji Bank.
他是富士银行的雇员。

situation [ˌsɪtʃuˈeɪʃn] *n.* （人的）情况；局面，形势，处境

例 Army officers said the situation was under control.
陆军军官称局面已经得到了控制。

victim [ˈvɪktɪm] *n.* 牺牲者，受害者

例 Not all the victims survived.
并非所有受害者都得以幸存。

protest [ˈprəʊtest] *n.* 抗议；断言 *vi.* 抗议；声明反对；断言

例 Groups of women took to the streets to protest against the arrests.
成群结队的妇女上街抗议逮捕行动。

junk [dʒʌŋk] *n.* 废旧物品，破烂物

例 There are racks of musty clothing and piles of junk.
有几架子发霉的衣物和成堆的废旧杂物。

语法知识点 *Grammar Points*

① **When someone would ask him how he was doing, he would reply, "If I were any better, I would be twins!"**

本句中运用if引导虚拟语气。If引导虚拟语气表示与将来事实相反有三种表达模式：if+主语+were to do / if+主语+should+do / if+主语+动词一般过去式（be动词用were）。

例 If he should come here tomorrow, I would talk to him.
如果他明天来这儿的话，我就跟他谈谈。

② **If an employee was having a bad day, Jerry was there telling the employee how to look on the positive side of the situation.**

本句中有固定短语look on...表示"观看，旁观；看待"。

例 A lot of people looked on him as a healer.
很多人视他为信仰疗法术士。

③ **The bottom line: It's your choice how you live life.**

本句中the bottom line表示"不得不接受的局面（事实）"。

> The bottom line is that it did not get the best out of everybody.
> 最关键的问题是这不能使每个人充分发挥自己的长处。

经典名句 Famous Classics

1. The secret of being miserable is to have leisure to bother about whether you are happy or not.
   痛苦的秘密在于有闲工夫担心自己是否幸福。

2. Optimists always picture themselves accomplishing their goals.
   乐观主义者总是想象自己实现了目标的情景。

3. Limitations live only in our minds. But if we use our imaginations, our possibilities become limitless.
   局限只存在于我们的大脑中。可是如果我们运用自己的想象力，就会获得无限的可能性。

4. The future is simply infinite possibility waiting to happen. What it waits on is human imagination to crystallize its possibilities.
   未来就是有待发生的可能性。它等待着人类的想象力将这些可能性明确化。

5. Some of the world's greatest feats were accomplished by people not smart enough to know they were impossible.
   世上有些丰功伟绩之所以能够缔造，是因为有些人不够"聪明"，不知道那些原是不可能的。

6. Young men make great mistakes in life; for one thing, they idealize love too much.
   年轻人一生中常犯大错误，其中之一就是把爱情太理想化了。

21 Dell's Story
戴尔的故事

On January 2, 1984, I went back to Austin earlier than I would have to attend classes, and I did all the things I need to do to set up a business. I **registered** the company with the State of Texas as "PC's Limited". I placed ads in the **classified** section in our local newspaper.

Through my previous **contract** with customers and the small ads I placed in the paper, I was already getting a lot of business. I was selling between $50,000 to $80,000 upgraded PCs, upgrade **kits** and add-on computer **components** to people in Austin area. Not long after starting the classes I was able to move from a **stuffy** room that I shared with a roommate to a **condominium** with high ceilings and two bedrooms. I didn't, however, tell my parents for a few months that I moved.

In early May, about a week before I took my final exam to complete my freshman year, I **incorporated** the company as "Dell Computer Corporation", doing business as "PC's Limited". We moved the business from my condo to a 1000-square-foot office

1984年1月2日，我开学前早一点回到了奥斯汀（德克萨斯州首府），我做好了成立新公司的前期准备。我注册的公司是德克萨斯州的"个人电脑有限公司"。我在当地报纸的分类广告中登了广告。

通过先前和客户签订的合同以及登在报纸上的小广告，我已经有了很多生意。我销售了50000到80000美元升级的个人电脑，升级套件和附加的电脑组件给奥斯汀地区的人们。开学后不久，我便从和室友共住的闷热宿舍搬出来，住进了一个高顶双卧的公寓套间。然而，我没有告诉我的父母我已经搬家几个月了。

5月初，在我完成大学一年级的期末考试的一周前，我将公司注册为"戴尔计算机公司"，从事"个人电脑有限公司"的业务。我们把办公场所从我的公寓搬到了位于北奥斯汀的一个小商业中心的一个1000平方英尺的办公室。我雇了几个人来接电话，并且安排另外几个人沟通订单。制造者

space in a small business center in North Austin. I hired a few people to take orders over telephone and a few more to fulfill them. **Manufacturing** consisted of three guys with **screwdrivers** sitting at six-foot tables upgrading machines. Business continued to grow, and I began to think of what the potential could be if I could devote myself to the **venture**, full-time.

Where I came from, not going to the college is not an acceptable option. Convincing my parents to allow me to leave school would have been impossible. So I just went ahead and did it, whatever the consequences would be. I finished my freshman year and left.

People asked me now, "Were you scared?" Sure.

But it turned out, the timing for "PC's Limited" couldn't have been better.

有三人，拿着螺丝刀坐在六英尺长的桌子旁升级电脑。生意继续发展，我开始考虑如果我能全身心投入到这项事业中，我的潜力会是什么。

我的出生决定了不去上大学不是一个可以接受的选择。说服父母允许我离开学校更是不可能的。所以我就提前这样做了，不管后果如何。我完成了大学一年级学业就离开了。

人们现在问我："你当时害怕吗？"当然。

而结果证明，那个时候成立"个人电脑有限公司"再好不过。

单词解析 Word Analysis

register ['redʒɪstə(r)] *vt.* 登记，注册

例 In order to register a car in Japan, the owner must have somewhere to park it.
在日本要登记一辆汽车，车主必须先要有车位。

classified ['klæsɪfaɪd] *adj.* 分类的，归类的

例 She never participated in obtaining or copying any classified documents for anyone.
她从未参与过任何人获取或复制机密文件之事。

Dell's Story 戴尔的故事 21

contract ['kɒntrækt] *v.* 签合同
- 例 You can contract with us to deliver your cargo.
  你可以跟我们签订送货合同。

kit [kɪt] *n.* 成套用品；配套元件
- 例 The kit consisted of about twenty cosmetic items and a lady's shaver.
  整套工具包括大约20种化妆用品和一个女士脱毛器。

component [kəm'pəʊnənt] *n.* 成分；组分；零件
- 例 Enriched uranium is a key component of a nuclear weapon.
  浓缩铀是核武器的关键组成部分。

stuffy ['stʌfi] *adj.* 闷热的，不通气的
- 例 It was hot and stuffy in the classroom.
  教室里很闷热。

condominium [ˌkɒndə'mɪniəm] *n.* 公寓；一套公寓住房；公寓的单元
- 例 Study on the Co-Ownership in the Condominium Ownership
  建筑物区分所有权中的共有权问题研究

incorporate [ɪn'kɔ:pəreɪt] *v.* 组成公司
- 例 We had to incorporate the company for tax reasons.
  由于纳税的原因，我们不得不把那家公司合并了。

corporation [ˌkɔ:pə'reɪʃn] *n.* 公司；法人；社团，团体
- 例 The rule applies where a person owns stock in a corporation.
  该规定适用于持有公司股票的人。

manufacturing [ˌmænju'fæktʃərɪŋ] *n.* 制造，生产工业
- 例 Managers have learned to grapple with networking, artificial intelligence, computer-aided engineering and manufacturing.
  经理们已经学会了如何应对联网、人工智能、计算机辅助工程和制造。

screwdriver ['skru:draɪvə(r)] *n.* 螺丝刀；螺丝起子
- 例 Dean tried to stab him with a screwdriver.
  迪安试图用一把改锥捅他。

venture ['ventʃə(r)] *n.* 冒险；冒险事业；冒险行动；商业冒险

例 "Don't ask," he said, whenever Ginny ventured to raise the subject.
每当金尼鼓起勇气提起这个话题时，他就说"不要问"。

语法知识点 Grammar Points

① **On January 2, 1984, I went back to Austin earlier than I would have to attend classes, and I did all the things I need to do to set up a business.**

本句中 set up 译为"建立；装配；开业；竖立"。

例 The two sides agreed to set up a commission to investigate claims.
双方同意组建一个委员会来调查那些索赔要求。

② **Not long after starting the classes I was able to move from a stuffy room that I shared with a roommate to a condominium with high ceilings and two bedrooms.**

本句中 not long after 表示"不久之后……"，为固定的表达方式。

例 Not long after his return, a local war broke out near his town.
他回到家乡后不久，一场区域性的战争在他家乡附近爆发了。

③ **But it turned out, the timing for "PC's Limited" couldn't have been better.**

本句中 turn out 表示"生产；结果是；关掉；出动；驱逐"。在该句之中为"结果是"的意思。

例 I knew it would turn out to be one of those days when I overslept.
我明白，如果我睡过头，那结果会是很不妙的。

经典名句 Famous Classics

1. Today, give a stranger one of your smiles. It might be the only sunshine he sees all day.
今天，给一个陌生人送上你的微笑吧，很可能这是他一天中见到的唯

Dell's Story
戴尔的故事 21

一的阳光。

2. Definition of best friend? They would let you KNOW when you had something in your teeth!
   什么叫最好的朋友？最好的朋友就是当你牙齿上有脏东西的时候，他们会立马提醒你。

3. If you have always done it that way, it is probably wrong.
   如果你一直用这种方法做事，那它很可能是错误的。

4. I cannot give you the formula for success, but I can give you the formula for failure, which is: Try to please everybody.
   我不能给你成功的计算公式，但我可以给你失败的计算公式，那就是：试着取悦每个人。

5. The wind direction is determined by the tree, the person's direction is determined by yourself.
   风的方向是由树决定，人的方向是由自己决定。

6. The waves to split the wind chopped waves ship farewell dinner, to go with the flow in the canoe of honor.
   海浪为劈风斩浪的航船饯行，为随波逐流的轻舟送葬。

7. Person without good faith, even if understanding ability, always just a dangerous man.
   人如果没有诚信，就算有聪明能力，也永远只是个危险人物。

读书笔记

22 Benefits from Occasional Stress
从偶尔的压力中受益

"Humans should not try to avoid stress any more than they would **shun** food, love or exercise." Said Dr. Hans Selye, the first **physician** to **document** the effects of stress on the body. While here's on question that continuous stress is harmful, several studies suggest that challenging situations in which you're able to rise to the occasion can be good for you.

In a 2001 study of 158 hospital nurses, those who faced considerable work demands but coped with the challenge were more likely to say they were in good health than those who felt they couldn't get the job done. In a study at the Academic Center for Dentistry in Amsterdam, researchers put volunteers through two stressful experiences. In the first, a timed task that required memorizing a list followed by a short test subjects through a **gory** video on surgical procedures. Those who did well on the memory test had an increase in levels of immunoglobulin A, an **antibody** that's the body's first line of **defense** against germs. The video-watchers experienced a downturn in the antibody.

汉斯·塞利博士——第一个研究记录压力对人体影响的医生，他曾说过："相较于节食、爱情及锻炼，人类不应该去过多躲避压力。"尽管大家都知道持续性压力是有害的，但一些研究表明挑战性的情形下你要是能够振作起来对你有好处。

在2001年一项研究158名医院护士的报告中，那些面临巨大工作要求但最终战胜挑战的护士比那些认为自己不胜任的护士健康状况更好。在阿姆斯特丹牙科医学学术中心的一项研究中，研究人员让志愿者度过两次充满压力的测试。首先，一个定时任务要求记录受试者通过观看对血腥的外科手术视频记忆过程。那些在记忆力测试中表现良好的人的免疫球蛋白A水平有所提高，这是机体抵御细菌的第一道防线。视频观察者的抗体下降了。

压力促使身体产生一定的应激激素。总之，这些激素有积极的作用，包括改善记忆功能。纽约洛克菲勒大学的布

Benefits from Occasional Stress
从偶尔的压力中受益 22

Stress **prompts** the body to produce certain stress hormones. In short these hormones have a positive effect, including improved memory function. "They can help nerve cells handle information and put it into storage, " says Dr. Bruce McEwen of Rockefeller University in New York. But in the long run these hormones can have a harmful effect on the body and brain.

"Sustained stress is not good for you, " says Richard Morimoto, a researcher at Northwestern University in Illinois studying the effects of stress on **longevity**, "It's the occasional burst of stress or brief exposure to stress that could be protective."

鲁斯·麦克尤恩博士说："它们可以帮助神经细胞处理信息并将其储存起来。"但从长远看，这些激素对大脑和身体都有不良影响。

"持续的压力对你的身体不好"，在伊利诺斯的学习压力对长寿的影响的西北大学研究员理查德·森本说道，"偶尔爆发的压力或短暂的压力可能是保护性的。"

单词解析 Word Analysis

shun [ʃʌn] *vt.* 避免；避开，回避
- From that time forward everybody shunned him.
  从那时候起，每个人都有意回避他。

physician [fɪ'zɪʃn] *n.* 医生，内科医生
- I committed the physician's cardinal sin: I got involved with my patients.
  我犯了从医的大忌：跟病人有了感情纠葛。

document ['dɒkjumənt] *vt.* 记录；证明；为……提供证明
- He wrote a book documenting his prison experiences.
  他写书详细记录了他的狱中经历。

gory [ˈgɔːri] *adj.* 沾满血污的，充满暴力和血腥的

例 I'm terribly squeamish. I can't bear gory films.
我非常容易受到惊吓。我受不了暴力血腥的电影。

antibody [ˈæntibɒdi] *n.* <医>抗体

例 I had the viral load and antibody tests.
我做了滤过性病毒填充和抗体测试。

defense [dɪˈfens] *vt.* 谋划抵御

例 Resistance to or defense against a hostile takeover.
对敌对占领的抵抗和抵御。

prompt [prɒmpt] *v.* 提示；促使；导致

例 If he gets stuck on a word, he can make the computer prompt him.
如果他被某个单词绊住，他可以从电脑上获得提示。

longevity [lɒnˈdʒevəti] *n.* 长寿；寿命；长期供职

例 I want to wish you longevity and health!
我希望你长寿和健康！

语法知识点 Grammar Points

① **Humans should not try to avoid stress any more than they would shun food, love or exercise.**

本句中固定短语any more than表示"较……多些"。

例 I'm not enthuse over my job any more than before.
我对工作不像以前那样热心了。

② **While here's on question that continuous stress is harmful, several studies suggest that challenging situations in which you're able to rise to the occasion can be good for you.**

该句子中包含了用in which引导的定语从句，先行词为situations。

③ **In a 2001 study of 158 hospital nurses, those who faced considerable work demands but coped with the challenge were more likely to say they were in good health than those who felt they couldn't fit the job done.**

本句中cope with表示"处理，应付"。

例 We can certainly cope with these enemy forces and even with larger ones.
我们当然对付得了这些敌军，甚至更多些也不在乎。

④ **Those who did well on the memory test had an increase in levels of immunoglobulin A, an antibody that's the body's first line of defense against germs.**

本句中who引导主语从句，who为关系代词。

例 Those who want to go please sign their names here.
想去的人在此签名。

⑤ **But in the long run these hormones can have a harmful effect on the body and brain.**

本句中in the long run表示"从长远看来"。

例 In the long run prices are bound to rise.
从长远看，物价肯定要涨。

经典名句 Famous Classics

1. If you fight for yourself, only you can win; when you fight for your marriage, you both win.
   如果你只为自己奋斗，只有你一个人是赢家；若为婚姻奋斗，夫妻两人都是赢家。

2. Treat other people as you hope they will treat you.
   你希望别人如何对待你，你就如何对待别人。

3. Imagination is more important than knowledge.
   想象力比知识更为重要。

4. I am a slow walker, but I never walk backwards.
   我走得很慢，但是我从来不会后退。

5. Enjoy the journey of life and not just the endgame.
   享受人生的旅途，而不是只有结果。

6. Nothing for nothing.
   不费力气，一无所得。

7. Better be the head of an ass than the tail of a horse.
   宁为鸡头，不为凤尾。

8. It's never too late to mend.
   过而能改，善莫大焉。（亡羊补牢，犹未晚也。）

读书笔记

23 We Never Told Him He Couldn't Do It
我们从不说他做不到

My son Joey was born with **club feet**. The doctors assured us that with treatment he would be able to walk normally — but would never run very well. The first three years of his life were spent in **surgery**, casts and **braces**. By the time he was eight, you wouldn't know he had a problem when you saw him walk.

The children in our neighborhood ran around as most children do during play, and Joey would jump right in and run and play, too. We never told him that he probably wouldn't be able to run as well as the other children. So he didn't know.

In seventh grade he decided to go out for the **cross-country** team. Every day he trained with the team. He worked harder and ran more than any of the others—perhaps he sensed that the abilities that seemed to come **naturally** to so many others did not come naturally to him. Although the entire team runs, only the top seven runners have the **potential** to score points for the school. We didn't tell him he probably would never make the team, so he didn't know.

我儿子乔伊出生时带有先天性畸形足。医生向我们保证，只要他接受治疗，他就能正常行走，但绝不会跑得很好。乔伊前三年的生活都花费在外科手术、打石膏和背带整形上。当他八岁的时候，你已经不会从他走路上看出问题。

邻居的小孩们做游戏的时候总是跑来跑过去，毫无疑问小乔伊看到他们玩就会马上加进去跑啊闹啊的。我们从来没有告诉过他，他可能没法和其他孩子跑得一样好。因此他并不知道。

七年级时，他决定参加越野队。每天他和团队一起训练。或许是他意识到许多本来应该和其他队友一样与生俱来的能力并没有体现在他身上，因此他比其他人更努力，跑得更多。尽管全队都在训练，但只有队里的前7名赛跑者可以代表学校参加比赛，为学校争光。我们没有告诉他，他可能永远也得不到名额，所以他不知道。

他坚持继续每天跑四到五英里，即使发高烧那天也没停

He continued to run four to five miles a day, every day — even the day he had a 103-degree fever. I was worried, so I went to look for him after school. I found him running all alone. I asked him how he felt. "Okay, " he said. He had two more miles to go. The **sweat** ran down his face and his eyes were glassy from his fever. Yet he looked **straight** ahead and kept running. We never told him he couldn't run four miles with a 103-degree fever. So he didn't know.

Two weeks later, the names of the team runners were called. Joey was number six on the list. Joey had made the team. He was in seventh grade—the other six team members were all eighth-graders. We never told him he shouldn't expect to make the team. We never told him he couldn't do it. We never told him he couldn't do it so he didn't know. He just did it.

下。我感觉非常担忧，所以我在他放学后去学校找他。我发现他独自一人跑着。我问他感觉如何。"很好！"他说道。他仍然还有两英里需要跑。汗水顺着他的脸颊流下，眼睛因为高烧而呆滞。但他直视前方，继续奔跑。我们从没告诉过他103华氏度高烧跑不了四英里。所以他不知道。

两周后，参赛组成员名单公布。乔伊名列排行榜第六位。乔伊成功得到了名额。他是七年级学生而其他六位成员都是八年级的学生。我们从来没有告诉他，他不要期望进入参赛组。我们从来没有告诉他，他不可能做到的。正因为我们从来没有说，所以他并不知道。他只是用行动去实现梦想。

单词解析 Word Analysis

club feet [klʌb fi:t] *n.* 畸形足，内外足（club foot的名词复数）

例 They talk about a new method for curing club feet.
这里介绍了治疗跛脚的最新方法。

surgery ['sɜ:dʒəri] *n.* 外科学，外科手术；手术室；诊所；诊断时间

例 His father has just recovered from heart surgery.
他父亲刚刚从心脏外科手术中康复过来。

We Never Told Him He Couldn't Do It
我们从不说他做不到

brace [breɪs] *n.* 支持物;铁钳,夹子

例 The odor of souls is a brace to the walls.
灵魂的气息是这些砖墙的支柱。

cross-country [ˈkrɔːsˈkʌntriː, ˈkrɔs-] *adj.* 越野的;横越全国的

例 She finished third in the world cross-country championships in Antwerp.
她在安特卫普的世界越野锦标赛上获得了第3名。

naturally [ˈnætʃrəli] *adv.* 自然地,表现自然地,顺理成章地;合理地

例 Some individuals are naturally good communicators.
一些人天生善于交流沟通。

potential [pəˈtenʃl] *n.* 潜力,潜能;[物]电位,势能;潜能的事物

例 The school strives to treat pupils as individuals and to help each one to achieve their full potential.
学校力求对每一个学生因材施教,帮助他们充分发挥其潜力。

sweat [swet] *n.* 汗水

例 Both horse and rider were dripping with sweat within five minutes.
没过五分钟,马和骑手都大汗淋漓。

straight [streɪt] *adv.* 直地;直接地;坦率地;立即

例 He finished his conversation and stood up, looking straight at me.
他说完话站起来,直视着我。

语法知识点 *Grammar Points*

① **The children in our neighborhood ran around as most children do during play, and Joey would jump right in and run and play, too.**

本句中run around 表示"东奔西跑;(特指孩子)到处玩耍游逛"。

例 Our teacher made us run around the track ten times!
我们的老师叫我们绕着跑道跑十圈!

② **Perhaps he sensed that the abilities that seemed to come naturally to so many others did not come naturally to him.**

本句中第一个 that 引导宾语从句，第二个 that 引导定语从句，先行词是 the abilities。

③ **Although the entire team runs, only the top seven runners have the potential to score points for the school.**

本句中 although 引导让步状语从句。

④ **The sweat ran down his face and his eyes were glassy from his fever.**

本句中固定短语 run down 表示"撞倒；使……变弱；停止；浏览；追溯"。在本句中为"流下"的意思。

例 Sweat ran down his face as he worked on.
他干活时脸上不断淌汗。

⑤ **Yet he looked straight ahead and kept running.**

本句中 look ahead 表示"向前看"；keep doing sth. 表示"继续做某事"。

例 I'm trying to look ahead at what might happen and be ready to handle it.
我打算未雨绸缪，做好应对准备。
I keep doing sign language, so I forget how to speak.
我一直做手语，我都不知道怎么说了。

经典名句 Famous Classics

1. Knowledge, in truth, is the great sun in the firmament. Life and power are scattered with all its beams.
   知识的确是天空中硕大无比的太阳，它的光辉撒下生命和力量。

2. That is a good book which is opened with expectation and closed with profit.
   好书使人开卷有所求，闭卷有所获。

3. There is no such thing as genius; it is nothing but labor and diligence.
   世间无所谓天才，它仅是刻苦加勤奋。

We Never Told Him He Couldn't Do It
我们从不说他做不到

4. The horizon of life is broadened chiefly by the enlargement of the heart.
   生活的地平线是随着心灵的开阔而变得宽广的。

5. If you should put even a little on a little, and should do this often, soon this too would become big.
   伟大的事业是通过不懈努力，一砖一瓦堆起来的。

6. The drop of rain makes a hole in the stone, not by violence, but by often falling.
   雨滴穿石，不是靠蛮力，而是靠持之以恒。

7. On life's earnest battle they only prevail, who daily march onward and never say fail.
   在顽强战斗中，只有每天不屈不挠奋勇向前的人才能取得胜利。

读书笔记

24 There Are No Such Setbacks That We Could Not Overcome
人生没有过不去的坎

Our **tolerating** ability is indeed way beyond our imagination. But not until the very critical moment will we realize our potential tolerating ability.

There was a woman in the countryside who got married at the age of 18 and had to escape with her two daughters and a son wherever she could at the age of 26 due to the Japanese army's **invasion**. Many people in the village at that time could not bear the suffering of being a **fugitive** and wanted to commit **suicide**. After she knew about it, she would come to those people and **soothed** them by saying, "Don't do that silly thing. There are no such **setbacks** that we could not overcome. The Japanese armies are bound to be foiled one day!"

After giving birth to the second son, her husband died of edema, which almost blew her away. But eventually, she recovered and cuddled the three young children, saying, "My sweet hearts, don't feel scared. You still have me, your dear mum!"

Nevertheless, the Heaven seemed to show no **affection** to her who had

人的承受能力，其实远远超乎我们的想象，就像不到关键时刻，我们很少能认识到自己的潜力有多大。

有这样一位农村妇女，她18岁的时候结婚，26岁赶上日本人侵略中国，在农村进行大扫荡，她不得不经常带着两个女儿一个儿子四处逃亡，东躲西藏。当时村里的许多人忍受不了逃亡的痛苦，想自杀。当她知道这件事情后，她就来到那些人身边说："别做那种傻事，没有什么挫折是我们无法克服的，日本鬼子总有一天会被打败的！"

生了第二个儿子后，她的丈夫因水肿而死，这几乎把她吓坏了。但最终，她从悲伤中恢复了，抱着三个年幼的孩子，说："我亲爱的孩子，你们不要害怕，你们还有我——你们亲爱的母亲。"

可是，上苍似乎并不眷顾这位一生坎坷的妇女。她在照顾孙子时意外地摔断了腿。由于她年事已高，给她做手术有很大的风险，她没有接受手

There Are No Such Setbacks That We Could Not Overcome
人生没有过不去的坎

undergone a rough life. She got her leg broken accidentally when she was nursing her grandson. Due to her old age that posed a great risk to her operation, she did not receive operation and had to lie in bed all day long. Her children all cried heavily, while she merely said, "Why do you cry? I am still living."

Even though she could not rise from bed, she did not complain about anything and anybody. Instead, she sat on the bed and did some stitching work. She had learnt scarves-weaving, **broidery**, crafts-making, etc. All her neighbors spoke highly of her skills and came to learn from her.

She lived until 86. Before she went to Heaven, she said to her children, "You all should live to your best. There are no such setbacks that we could not overcome!"

We will only get to realize our own iron will and strong tolerating ability after getting **stricken** heavily. Therefore, no matter what you are suffering from now, do not merely complain about the unfairness of our destiny and maintain low-spirited all the time. There are no such setbacks that we couldn't overcome. Only those who have no confidence and courage to overcome setbacks will be defeated at last!

术，不得不整天躺在床上。她的孩子们都哭得很厉害，而她只是说："你们为什么哭？我还活着呢。"

虽然她不能起床，但她并没有抱怨任何事和任何人。相反，她坐在床上做针线活。她已经学会了编织围巾、刺绣、工艺品制作等。她的邻居们都高度赞扬她的技巧，并向她学习。

她活到86岁。在她去世之前，她对她的孩子们说："你们都应该尽力而为。没有什么挫折是我们无法克服的！"

我们只有在遭受重创之后才能意识到自己的钢铁意志和强大的承受能力。所以，无论你现在遭受什么，不要只抱怨我们命运的不公平而一直保持低潮。人生没有过不去的坎。只有那些没有信心和勇气战胜挫折的人才最终会被打败！

单词解析 *Word Analysis*

tolerate ['tɒləreɪt] *vt.* 忍受；容许；承认；容忍

例 She can no longer tolerate the position that she's in.
她再也受不了自己的处境了。

invasion [ɪn'veɪʒn] *n.* 侵袭；入侵，侵略；侵害，侵犯

例 He was commander in chief during the invasion of Panama.
在侵略巴拿马的战役中他是总司令。

fugitive ['fju:dʒətɪv] *n.* 逃命者；难捕捉之物

例 The rebel leader was a fugitive from justice.
叛军头目是一名在逃的不法之徒。

suicide ['su:ɪsaɪd] *n.* 自杀；自杀行为；自杀者

例 Quite a few have committed social suicide by writing their boring memoirs.
有一些人因为写那些枯燥无味的回忆录而毁了自己的社会形象。

soothe [su:ð] *vt.* 安慰；缓和；使平静；减轻痛苦

例 He would take her in his arms and soothe her.
他将她拥入怀中抚慰她。

setback ['setbæk] *n.* 挫折；退步；阻碍；逆流

例 The move represents a setback for the Middle East peace process.
这个行动意味着中东和平进程受挫。

affection [ə'fekʃn] *n.* 喜爱，慈爱；情感或感情；意向；疾病，病情

例 She had developed quite an affection for the place.
她逐渐对这个地方钟爱有加。

broidery [b'rɔɪdərɪ] *n.* <古，诗>刺绣

例 She had learnt scarves-weaving, broidery, crafts-making, etc. All her neighbors spoke highly of her skills and came to learn from her.
她会织围巾，会绣花，会编手工艺品，左邻右舍的人都夸她手艺好，还来跟她学艺。

There Are No Such Setbacks That We Could Not Overcome 24
人生没有过不去的坎

stricken ['strɪkən] v. 打击（strike的过去分词）

例 The attacker struck as she was walking near a housing estate at Monacurra
她走到莫纳卡拉的一个居民区附近时遭人攻击。

语法知识点 Grammar Points

① There was a woman in the countryside who got married at the age of 18 and had to escape with her two daughters and a son wherever she could at the age of 26 due to the Japanese army's invasion.

本句中 who 引导从句，先行词 a woman；固定短语 due to，意为"由于，应归于"。

例 Unfortunately, due to unforeseen circumstances, this year's show has been cancelled.
遗憾的是，由于一些意外情况，今年的演出被取消了。

② The Japanese armies are bound to be foiled one day!

本句中 be bound to 为固定搭配，表示"注定；一定要……；终归；不得不"的意思。

例 If this is set to Bind, then the data will simply be bound to the control.
如果它被设置成了Bind，那么数据就会简单地绑定至控件。

③ Nevertheless, the Heaven seemed to show no affection to her who had undergone a rough life.

本句中 nevertheless 意为"然而，可是"，表达一种转折。

例 Most marriages fail after between five and nine years. Nevertheless, people continue to get married.
大部分婚姻在婚后第五至第九年间失败，然而，人们仍会选择结婚。

④ There are no such setbacks that we couldn't overcome.

本句是由that 引导的定语从句，先行词为 setbacks，整句译为"人生没有过不去的坎"。

经典名句 Famous Classics

1. All that you do, do with your might; things done by halves are never done right.
一切事情都应尽力而为，不可半途而废。

2. For all pain helps to make us rise, however much we may hate it at the time.
一切痛苦都有助于我们奋发向上，不论我们当时是多么憎恨它。

3. Life is a test and this world a place of trial. Always the problems — or it may be the same problem will be presented to every generation in different forms.
人生是一种考验，而这个世界就是考场。每一代都要面对一些问题——可能是相同的问题——只不过问题的形式不同。

4. Wish you an endless view to cheer your eyes, then one more story mount and higher rise.
欲穷千里目，更上一层楼。

5. Nothing in the world is difficult for one who sets his mind on it.
世上无难事，只怕有心人。

6. Man cannot discover new oceans unless he has courage to lose sight of the shore.
人只有鼓起勇气，告别海岸，才能发现新的海洋。

读书笔记

25 Shower Brings Flowers
骤雨带来似锦繁花

From the golden-tipped fields of mid-west America to the **ancient** kingdoms of **verdant** Palestine, there is a happy truth to be shared with all who would take heed.

In more recent times, this truth has been expressed as: April showers bring May flowers. This is a truth that promises light **bursting** from darkness, strength born from weakness and, if one dares to believe, life emerging from death.

Farmers all over the world know the importance and **immutability** of the seasons. They know that there is a season to plant and a season to **harvest**; everything must be done in its own time. Although the rain pours down with the **utmost relentlessness**, ceasing all outdoor activities, the man of the field lifts his face to the heavens and smiles. Despite the **inconvenience**, he knows that the rain provides the **nourishment** his crops need to grow and **flourish**. The **torrential** rains in the month of April, give rise to the glorious flowers in the month of May.

But this ancient truth applies to more than the crops of the fields; it is an

从美国中西部金色的田野，到巴勒斯坦嫩绿色的古老疆土，那些留心观察的人共享着同一个快乐真理。

近来这一真理被阐述为：四月的雨带来五月的花。这一真理预示光明会从黑暗中迸发；刚强生自软弱；如果你敢确信，生命会从死亡中萌发！

全世界的农民们都明白季节的重要性和永恒性。他们知道在哪个季节播种，哪个季节收获，每件事都必须应时而做！虽然暴雨无情地倾盆而下，迫使所有的户外劳作停止，但土地的主人会仰天微笑。尽管有诸多不便，但是他知道，雨会为他的庄稼带来繁茂生长所需的营养。四月里的豪雨，会带来五月里的繁花似锦。

但是这一古老真理并不只适用于田里的庄稼，它还是那些正经历着人生磨难的人的无限希冀：一段友谊的受挫会开启另一段崭新友谊的大门；此处失去的工作会提供彼处更好的工作机会；一个梦想的破灭会成为美好未来的基石。万物

invaluable message of hope to all who experience tragedy in life. A dashed relationship with one can open up the door to a brand new friendship with another. A lost job here can provide the opportunity for a better job there. A broken dream can become the **foundation** of a wonderful future. Everything has its place.

Remember this: overwhelming darkness may endure for a night, but it will never overcome the **radiant** light of the morning. When you are in a season of sorrow, hang in there, because a season of joy may be just around the corner…

皆有道！

请谨记：势不可挡的黑暗或有一晚，但它永远无法阻挡清晨的万丈光芒！当你正处于悲伤之季，请坚持住，因为欢乐的季节也许马上就会到来……

单词解析 Word Analysis

ancient ['eɪnʃənt] *adj.* 古代的；古老的，老式的

例 They believed ancient Greece and Rome were vital sources of learning.
他们认为古代希腊罗马是知识的重要发源地。

verdant ['vɜ:dnt] *adj.* 嫩绿的；（草、田地等）翠绿的

例 The verdant mountain forest turns red gradually in the autumn wind.
苍翠的山林在秋风中渐渐变红了。

burst [bɜ:st] *v.* 充满；爆炸；冲破，胀破

例 A dam burst and flooded their villages.
堤坝决口，淹没了他们的村庄。

immutability [ɪ,mju:tə'bɪlətɪ] *n.* 不变，不变性，永恒性

例 The president stressed once more the immutability of his country's borders.
总统再次强调了国家的边界不可改变。

Shower Brings Flowers
骤雨带来似锦繁花 25

harvest ['hɑːvɪst] *n.* 收割；收成；收获季节；结果

例 Millions of people are threatened with starvation as a result of drought and poor harvests.
几百万人因干旱和歉收而受到饥饿的威胁。

utmost ['ʌtməʊst] *adj.* 极度的，最大的，最远的

例 It is a matter of the utmost urgency to find out what has happened to these people.
当务之急是要弄清楚这些人出了什么事。

relentlessness [rɪ'lentləsnəs] *n.* 无情

例 Although the rain pours the utmost relentlessness, ceasing all outdoor activities, the farmers are more than excited.
尽管无休止的倾盆大雨迫使所有户外劳作停止，但农民会为此兴奋不已。

inconvenience [ˌɪnkən'viːniəns] *n.* 麻烦；不方便

例 We apologize for any inconvenience caused during the repairs.
我们为维修期间造成的任何不便道歉。

nourishment ['nʌrɪʃmənt] *n.* 食物；滋养品，营养品

例 The mother provides the embryo with nourishment and a place to grow.
母亲为胎儿提供营养和成长的空间。

flourish ['flʌrɪʃ] *v.* 挥舞；茂盛，繁荣

例 The plant flourishes particularly well in slightly harsher climates.
这种植物在气候条件稍差一点的地区长势尤其好。

torrential [tə'renʃl] *adj.* 似急流的，猛烈的，汹涌的

例 It had been a night of stormy weather, with torrential rain and high winds.
这是一个暴风雨之夜，大雨倾盆，强风呼啸。

foundation [faʊn'deɪʃn] *n.* 基础；地基；粉底

例 The issue strikes at the very foundation of our community.
这个问题严重影响了我们社会的基本根基。

radiant ['reɪdɪənt] *adj.* 辐射的；容光焕发的；照耀的

例 The evening sun warms the old red brick wall to a radiant glow.
夕阳为古老的红砖墙罩上了一层暖暖的炫目光辉。

语法知识点 *Grammar Points*

① **This is a truth that promises light bursting from darkness, strength born from weakness and, if one dares to believe, life emerging from death.**

本句是由 that 引导的定语从句，先行词在从句中做主语成分，that 不可省略；burst from 表示"迸发"；born from 表示"出生于"；emerge from 表示"来自；浮现"。

例 A cry of anguish burst from her lips.
她突然痛苦地大叫了一声。
His voice stopped as he saw the blade emerge from Desmond's pocket.
当他看到从德斯蒙德口袋里露出的刀刃时，他突然不吭声了。

② **Although the rain pours down with the utmost relentlessness, ceasing all outdoor activities, the man of the field lifts his face to the heavens and smiles.**

本句是由 although 引导的让步状语从句，表示"虽然，尽管"，although 引导的让步状语从句一般放于句首的情况较多。

例 Although he is known to only a few, his reputation among them is very great.
虽然知道他的人不多，但他在这些人中名声却很响。
Although I was only six, I can remember seeing it on TV.
虽然那时我只有6岁，我依然记得在电视上见过它。

lift one's face 表示"把脸抬起来"。

例 I am your husband so lift your face up a little.
我是你的丈夫，所以把脸抬起来一些。

③ **The torrential rains in the month of April, give rise to the glorious flowers in the month of May.**

本句中 give rise to 表示"造成；引起，导致"。

例 There are a couple of factors that give rise to this problem.
有很多因素导致了这个问题。

Temperature dependence. That's, what can give rise to problems.
温度的依赖带来了这个问题。

经典名句 Famous Classics

1. If you don't fight for what you want, don't cry for what you lose.
   如果你想要却不去拼搏，那么失去了你就别哭泣。

2. We all have moments of desperation. But if we can face them head on, that's when we find out just how strong we really are.
   我们都有绝望的时候，只有在勇敢面对时，我们才知道我们有多坚强。

3. Be alike flower. Spread beauty and happiness wherever you stay; irrespective of your surroundings.
   像花儿一样，无论身在何处，不管周遭环境如何，都依然潇洒地绽放自己的美丽，活出自己的精彩。

4. A person in the world must have his own business, no matter big or small. Only with recognition from the society can your life be meaningful.
   人生在世总要做出一番事业，不管事业是大是小，总要让社会承认你的价值才不算枉活一世。

5. There is always a time in life, full of fear, but in addition to the courage to face, we have no choice.
   生命中总有那么一段时光，充满恐惧，可是除了勇敢面对，我们别无选择。

6. The best, not necessarily the most appropriate; the most appropriate, is really the best.
   最好的，不一定是最合适的；最合适的，才是真正最好的。

26 The Road to Success
成功之路

It is well that young men should begin at the beginning and occupy the most **subordinate** positions. Many of the leading businessmen of Pittsburgh had a serious responsibility thrust upon them at the very **threshold** of their career. They were introduced to the **broom**, and spent the first hours of their business lives sweeping out the office.

Assuming that you have all obtained employment and are fairly started, my advice to you is "aim high". I would not give a fig for the young man who does not already see himself the partner or the head of an important firm. Do not rest content for a moment in your thoughts as head clerk, or **foreman**, or general manager in any concern, no matter how extensive. Say to yourself, "My place is at the top." Be king in your dreams.

And here is the prime condition of success, the great secret: concentrate your energy, thought, and capital **exclusively** upon the business in which you are engaged. Having begun in one line, resolve to fight it out on that line, to lead in it, adopt every improvement, have the best machinery, and know the

年轻人应该从头学起，担当最基层的职务，这是件好事。匹兹堡有许多大企业家在创业之初都肩负过重任。他们与扫帚结伴，以清扫办公室度过了企业生涯的最初时光。

假如你已被录用，并有了一个良好的开端，我对你们的忠告是"要胸怀大志"。对那些尚未把自己看成是某重要公司的合伙人或领导人的年轻人，我会不屑一顾。你们在思想上一刻也不要满足于充当任何企业的首席职员、领班或总经理，不管这家企业的规模有多大。你们要对自己说；"我的位置在最高处。"你们要梦寐以求登峰造极。

获得成功的首要条件和最大秘诀是：把精力和财力完全集中于所干的事业上。一旦开始干那一行，就要决心干出个名堂，要出类拔萃，要点点滴滴地改进，要采用最好的机器，要尽力通晓这一行。

一些企业失败就在于分散了资金，因为这就意味着分散了精力。他们向这方面投资，

most about it.

The concerns which fail are those which have **scattered** their capital, which means that they have scattered their brains also. They have investments in this, or that, or the other, here there, and everywhere. "Don't put all your eggs in one basket." is all wrong. I tell you to "put all your eggs in one basket, and then watch that basket." Look round you and take notice, men who do that not often fail. It is easy to watch and carry the one basket. It is trying to carry too many baskets that breaks most eggs in this country. One fault of the American businessman is lack of concentration.

To summarize what I have said: aim for the highest; never enter a bar room; do not touch **liquor**, or if at all only at meals; never **speculate**; never **indorse** beyond your **surplus** cash fund; concentrate; put all your eggs in one basket, and watch that basket; **expenditure** always within **revenue**; lastly, be not impatient, for as Emerson says, "no one can cheat you out of **ultimate** success but yourselves."

又向那方面投资，方方面面都有投资。"别把所有的鸡蛋放进一只篮子"之说大错特错。我告诉你们，"要把所有的鸡蛋放进一只篮子，然后照管好那只篮子。"看看你周围，你就会注意到，能这样做的人往往不会失败。看管和携带一只篮子并不难，难的是试图携带多只篮子，从而打碎这个国家的大部分鸡蛋。美国商人的一个缺点就是不够专注。

我把所说的话归纳如下：要志存高远；千万不要涉足酒吧，不要沾酒，或者仅在用餐时喝点酒；千万不要投机；签署支付的款项时，千万不要超过盈余的现金储备；集中精力，把所有鸡蛋放进一只篮子并照管好那只篮子；支出永远小于收入；最后，不要失去耐心，因为正如爱默生所说："除了你自己以外，没有人能哄骗你离开最后的成功。"

单词解析 Word Analysis

subordinate [sə'bɔːdɪnət] *adj.* 下级的；级别或职位较低的；次要的；附属的

例 Sixty of his subordinate officers followed his example.
他的60个下级官员都以他为榜样。

threshold ['θreʃhəʊld] *n.* 门槛，入口，开始

例 He stopped at the threshold of the bedroom.
他在卧室门口停住了。

broom [bruːm] *n.* 扫帚

例 Norma picked up the broom and began sweeping.
诺尔玛拿起扫帚开始扫了起来。

foreman ['fɔːmən] *n.* 工头，领班；首席陪审员

例 He still visited the dairy daily, but left most of the business details to his manager and foreman.
他仍然每天到乳品场看看，但把生意上大部分琐碎事务交给经理和工头打理。

exclusively [ɪk'skluːsɪvlɪ] *adv.* 唯一地；专门地，特定地；专有地；排外地

例 Instruction in these subjects in undergraduate classes is almost exclusively by lecture.
本科生的这几门课程几乎完全是通过讲座教授的。

scatter ['skætə(r)] *v.* （使）散开，（使）分散，驱散；分散；撒开

例 She tore the rose apart and scattered the petals over the grave.
她掰开玫瑰花，将花瓣撒在坟墓上。

liquor ['lɪkə(r)] *n.* 酒，烈性酒；含酒精饮料

例 The room was filled with cases of liquor.
房间里堆满了整箱整箱的烈性酒。

speculate ['spekjʊleɪt] *v.* 猜测，推测；投机；思索

例 Critics of the project speculate about how many hospitals could be built instead.

对该项目持批评态度的人在推测如果改作他用不知可以建多少所医院。

indorse [ɪn'dɔːs] v. 签名于票据等的背面，认可

例 Flat-dwellers shall indorse my dictum that theirs is the only true happiness.
公寓生活是唯一真正的快乐，住公寓的人一定都赞成我的论断。

surplus ['sɜːpləs] adj. 过剩的；多余的

例 Germany suffers from a surplus of teachers.
德国遭遇了教师过剩的问题。

expenditure [ɪk'spendɪtʃə(r)] n. 花费，支出；费用，经费；（尤指金钱的）支出额

例 Policies of tax reduction must lead to reduced public expenditure.
减税政策必然导致公共支出的削减。

revenue ['revənjuː] n. 收益；财政收入；税收收入

例 Revenue from brown goods, including televisions and hi-fis, rose nearly 12 percent.
包括电视机和高保真音响在内的黑色家电的销售收入增加了将近12%。

ultimate ['ʌltɪmət] adj. 极限的；最后的；最大的；首要的

例 He said it is still not possible to predict the ultimate outcome.
他说现在还无法预料最终的结局。

语法知识点 Grammar Points

① **Assuming that you have all obtained employment and are fairly started, my advice to you is "aim high".**

本句中 assume that... 表示"假定，假设"。

例 But assuming that the talks make progress, won't they do too little, too late?
就算会谈取得了进展，也未免太微不足道，且为时太晚了吧？

② **I would not give a fig for the young man who does not already see himself the partner or the head of an important firm.**

本句是由 who 引导的定语从句,先行词 the young man;who 引导从句时,一般指人或这人格化的事物。

例 We are badly in need of those who can work in real earnest.
我们迫切需要能认真工作的人。

③ **The concerns which fail are those which have scattered their capital, which means that they have scattered their brains also.**

本句较长,句子的主干为:The concerns ... are those ...;本句中第一个 which 引导定语从句,先行词是 the concerns;第二个 which 先行词是 those,此处可用 who 替代,第三个 which 引导前面整个句子;后面 that 引导的定语从句,此处 that 可省略。

④ **Look round you and take notice, men who do that not often fail.**

本句中有两个固定短语,look around 表示"环顾四周",take notice 表示"注意观察"。

例 We went to look round the show homes.
我们去参观了一下样板间。
We want the government to take notice of what we think they should do for single parents.
我们希望政府能够关注单亲父母,为他们做一些应该做的事。

经典名句 Famous Classics

1. Don't aim for success if you want it; just do what you love and believe in, and it will come naturally.
如果你想要成功,不要去追求成功;尽管做你自己热爱的事情并且相信它,成功自然到来。

2. The man who has made up his mind to win will never say "impossible".
凡是决心取得胜利的人是从来不说"不可能的"。

The Road to Success
成功之路 26

3. Live a noble and honest life. Reviving past times in your old age will help you to enjoy your life again.
   过一种高尚而诚实的生活。当你年老时回想起过去，你就能再一次享受人生。

4. You cannot improve your past, but you can improve your future. Once time is wasted, life is wasted.
   你不能改变你的过去，但你可以让你的未来变得更美好。一旦时间浪费了，生命就浪费了。

5. Knowledge is a city to the building of which every human being brought a stone.
   知识是一座城堡，每个人都应为它增砖添瓦。

6. Real knowledge, like everything else of value, is not to be obtained easily, it must be worked for, studied for, thought for, and more than all, must be prayed for.
   真知如同珍宝，不是轻易获得的，必须学习、钻研、思考，最重要的是必须有强烈的求知欲。

7. Knowledge makes humble, ignorance makes proud.
   知识使人谦虚，无知使人骄傲。

读书笔记

27 Sleeping Through the Storm
未雨绸缪

It was spring, in western America, the weather was getting warmer. There was a young man who went out to find a job on a farm. He came to a small farm, which belonged to an old farmer and his wife. He told the farmer he wanted to apply for a job as a **farmhand**. When the farmer asked for his **qualifications**, "What can you do, boy?" the young man said, "I can sleep when the wind blows."

The answer quite **puzzled** the farmer and his wife. But he looked honest and reliable, so the couple decided to hire him.

Two months passed and the young man had worked well on the farm, nothing unusual.

One night, the farmer and his wife were awakened by a **violent** storm. They quickly began to check things out to see if all was secure. They found that the shutters of the farmhouse had been securely **fastened**. A good supply of **logs** had been set next to the fireplace.

The young man slept soundly.

The farmer and his wife then **inspected** their property. They found that the farm tools had been placed in the

春天到了，在美国西部，天气越来越暖和了。有一个年轻人去农场找工作。他来到一个属于一个老农夫和他妻子的小农场。他告诉农夫，他想做一个农场工人。当时农民问他有何资质，"你能做什么，孩子？"年轻人说："当暴风来临时，我可以安然入睡。"

这个答案使农夫和他的妻子十分困惑。但他看起来诚实可靠，所以这对夫妇决定雇佣他。

两个月过去了，这个年轻人在农场工作得很好，没有什么不寻常的。

一天晚上，农夫和他的妻子被暴风雨惊醒了。他们赶快检查想知道是不是一切都安然无恙。他们发现农舍的百叶窗已经牢固地固定起来了，壁炉旁边放了一大堆原木。

年轻人在呼呼大睡。

农夫和他的妻子随后检查了他们的财产。他们发现农具被放置在仓库里，远离风雨。拖拉机已经开进车库了。谷仓被锁好了。甚至动物也很平

Sleeping Through the Storm
未雨绸缪

storage shed, safe from the elements. The tractor had been moved into the garage. The **barn** was properly locked. Even the animals were calm. All was well.

The farmer then understood the meaning of the young man's words, "I can sleep when the wind blows." Because the farmhand did his work loyally and **faithfully** when the skies were clear, he was prepared for the storm when it broke. So when the wind blew, he was not afraid. He could sleep in peace.

We appreciate people who arrange their work well, who always make preparation in advance. Maybe we can use our spare time to do things just for fun, and then we work hard at work time. But those who prepare their work in advance would always have more chance to make work done well.

A work you prepared in advance, may save you from a **misfortune**.

静。一切都很好。

农夫明白了年轻人的话的含义："当暴风来临时，我可以安然入睡。"年轻人忠诚老实地做好自己的农场工作，当天气晴朗的时候，他为暴风来临而做好准备工作。因此当真正的暴风来临时，他不会觉得担忧并且可以安然入睡。

我们欣赏那些把自己的工作安排得很好的人，那些懂得未雨绸缪的人。也许我们可以利用业余时间做一些有趣的事情，然后我们在工作时间努力工作。但是那些提前准备工作的人总是有更多的机会让工作做得更好。

提前做好准备可以帮你避免厄运。

单词解析 Word Analysis

farmhand [ˈfɑːmhænd] *n.* 农业工人，农场工人，雇农

例 "Are you a good farmhand?" the farmer asked him.
"你是个干农活的好手吗？"农场主问他。

qualification [ˌkwɒlɪfɪˈkeɪʃn] *n.* 资格，授权；条件，限制；合格证书

例 Following qualification, he worked as a social worker.
通过资格考试认证之后，他做了一名社会工作者。

puzzled ['pʌzld] *adj.* 困惑的，糊涂的，茫然的

例 Critics remain puzzled by the British election results.
批评家仍然对英国大选的结果困惑不解。

violent ['vaɪələnt] *adj.* 暴力引起的；剧烈的，（风、爆炸等）猛烈的，狂暴的；（感情、颜色）强烈的

例 A quarter of current inmates have committed violent crimes.
现在关押的犯人中有1/4是暴力犯罪。

log [lɒg] *n.* 日志；记录；原木

例 He dumped the logs on the big stone hearth.
他将一根根短木柴扔进巨大的石壁炉里。

barn [bɑːn] *n.* 牲口棚；谷仓，粮仓；（公共汽车、卡车等的）车库

例 He and Walker patched the barn roof.
他和沃克补好了谷仓顶。

inspect [ɪn'spekt] *v.* 视察；检查，检验；进行检查；进行视察

例 Elaine went outside to inspect the playing field
伊莱恩走到外面查看操场。

faithfully ['feɪθfəli] *adv.* 忠实地；如实地；诚心诚意地

例 Our country has always adhered faithfully to the Five Principles of Peaceful Coexistence.
对于和平共处五项原则，我国一贯是恪守不渝的。

misfortune [ˌmɪsˈfɔːtʃuːn] *n.* 不幸；厄运；灾难；不幸的事

例 She seemed to enjoy the misfortunes of others.
她似乎喜欢幸灾乐祸。

语法知识点 Grammar Points

① He came to a small farm, which belonged to an old farmer and his wife.

本句是由 which 引导的非限定性定语从句，此处不能用 that 替代。

Sleeping Through the Storm
未雨绸缪 27

② **I can sleep when the wind blows.**

本句是由 when 引导的时间状语从句，表示"当……时候"。

③ **They quickly began to check things out to see if all was secure.**

本句中固定短语 check out 表示"检验；结账离开；通过考核；盖章"。

例 Maybe we ought to go down to the library and check it out.
或许我们应该去趟图书馆，查个明白。

④ **We appreciate people who arrange their work well, who always make preparation in advance.**

本句中包含两个由 who 引导的定语从句，先行词为 people。

⑤ **But those who prepare their work in advance would always have more chance to make work done well.**

本句中 who 引导定语从句，修饰先行词 those。

经典名句 Famous Classics

1. It takes anyone to stand by your side at your best. But it takes a special one to stand by your side at your worst.
   在你鼎盛的时候，任何人都可能站在你这边；但在你最低落的时候，站在你身边的只有那个特别的人。

2. If you don't know where you are going, any road will get you there.
   心中无路，则无处不达。

3. I want you to know that someone out there cares.
   要记得，你总会被牵挂。

4. Life is too ironic to fully understand. It takes sadness to know what happiness is, noise to appreciate silence and absence to value presence.
   人生总是充满讽刺，让人费解。总要伤了心，才明白什么是快乐；总要喧哗后，才懂得宁静难得；总要有些人不在了，才发现他/她在身边有多珍贵。

5. In the end you'll see who's fake, who's true and who would risk it all just for you.
   到最后，你总会明白，谁是虚情假意，谁是真心实意，谁为了你不顾一切。

6. Be thankful that you don't already have everything you desire. If you did, what would there be to look forward to?
   感谢你没有渴求到的一切东西，如果得到了你就不会再有期待。

读书笔记

28 Seek the Seed of Triumph in Everyday Adversity
梅花香自苦寒来

There is no better school than adversity. Every defeat, every **heartbreak**, every loss, contains its own seed, its own lesson on how to improve my **performance** next time. Never again will I **contribute** to my **downfall** by refusing to face the truth and learn from my past mistakes. Because I know: gems cannot shine without **polish**, and I cannot perfect myself without hardship.

Always will I seek the seed of triumph in every **adversity**.

I am better prepared, now, to deal with any adversity. No matter what fate has in store for me to know that I will relish it or I will suffer it for only a brief time. So very few understand this obvious truth while the rest allow their hopes and goals to vanish as soon as **tragedy** strikes. These unfortunately people carry with them, until they die their own bed of **thorns** and look to others. Every day, for sympathy and attention. Adversity will never destroy the person with courage and faith.

Always will I seek the seed of **triumph** in every adversity.

Now I know that there are no times in life when opportunity, the chance

逆境是一所最好的学校。每一次失败，每一次打击，每一次损失，都孕育着成功的萌芽，都教会我在下一次有更出色的表现。我再也不会逃避现实，也不会拒绝从以往的错误中获取经验，我不再因此而促成自己的失败。因为我知道，宝玉不经磨砺就不能发光，没有磨难我也不能完善自我。

我将一直在困境中寻找成功的希望。

现在我已经做好准备，去对抗逆境。无论我今后面对什么样的命运，我都将细细品味，痛苦也会很快过去。只有少数人知道这个显而易见的真理，其他人一旦悲剧降临，希望和目标就消失得无影无踪了。这些不幸的人至死都在苦难的深渊中，每天如坐针毡，祈求别人的同情和关注。逆境从来不会摧毁那些有勇气有信心的人。

我将一直在困境中寻找成功的希望。

现在我知道，灵魂倍受煎熬的时刻，也正是生命中最多选择与机会的时刻。任何

to be and do gathers so richly about my soul as when it has to suffer **cruel** adversity. Then everything depends on whether I raise my head or lower it in seeking help. Whenever I am struck down, in the future, by any terrible **defeat**, I will inquire of myself, after the first pain has passed, how I can turn that adversity into good. What a great opportunity that moment may present...to make the bitter root I am holding and transform it into **fragrant** garden of flowers.

Always will I seek the seed of triumph in every adversity.

事情的成败取决于我在寻求帮助时是抬起头还是低下头。无论何时，当我被可怕的失败击倒，在最初的阵痛过去之后，我都要想方设法将苦难变成好事。伟大的机遇就在这一刻闪现，这苦涩的根必将迎来满园芬芳！

我将一直在困境中寻找成功的希望。

单词解析 Word Analysis

heartbreak ['hɑːtbreɪk] *n.* 心碎，断肠；极度伤心

例 Recent events had obviously been a heartbreak for him.
最近发生的一系列事件显然让他伤心不已。

performance [pəˈfɔːməns] *n.* 表现；表演；演技；执行

例 Inside the theatre, they were giving a performance of Bizet's *Carmen*.
在剧院里，他们正在演出比才的作品《卡门》。

contribute [kənˈtrɪbjuːt] *v.* 贡献出；捐赠（款项）

例 The three sons also contribute to the family business.
这3个儿子也为家族事业做出了贡献。

downfall [ˈdaʊnfɔːl] *n.* 垮台

例 His lack of experience had led to his downfall.
经验不足导致了他的下台。

Seek the Seed of Triumph in Everyday Adversity
梅花香自苦寒来

polish ['pɒlɪʃ] *n.* 光泽剂，擦亮剂；擦亮，磨光
例 The still air smelt faintly of furniture polish.
凝滞的空气中隐隐有股家具上光剂的味道。

adversity [əd'vɜːsəti] *n.* 逆境；不幸；灾难
例 They had to struggle against all kinds of adversity.
他们不得不同一切困境做斗争。

tragedy ['trædʒədi] *n.* 悲剧，惨剧；悲剧文学
例 They have suffered an enormous personal tragedy.
他们遭逢了巨大的个人不幸。

thorns [θɔːnz] *n.* 荆棘；棘刺
例 Roses will always have thorns but with care they can be avoided.
玫瑰花上都有刺，不过只要小心就碰不到。

triumph ['traɪʌmf] *n.* 胜利；巨大的成就
例 The championships proved to be a personal triumph for the coach, Dave Donovan.
事实证明，在这次锦标赛中教练戴夫·多诺万取得了非凡的个人成就。

cruel [kruːəl] *adj.* 残酷的，残忍的
例 By a cruel irony, his horse came down on a flat part of the course.
十分残酷而且极具讽刺意味的是，他的马在赛场的平地上摔倒了。

defeat [dɪˈfiːt] *n.* 失败
例 There were times when the challenges of writing such a huge novel almost defeated her.
有些时候，创作如此宏大的一部小说所面临的挑战几乎把她给难倒了。

fragrant ['freɪɡrənt] *adj.* 芳香的，香的；愉快的
例 The air was fragrant with the smell of orange blossoms.
空气里弥漫着橘子花的香气。

语法知识点 Grammar Points

① Always will I seek the seed of triumph in every adversity.

本句属于部分倒装语序，以频度副词always, usually, often, now and then, many a time, every day等位于句首。表示强调时，用部分倒装；若不强调时，也可不用倒装。

例 Often did we warn him not to do so.
我曾常常警告他不要那样做。

② No matter what fate has in store for me to know that I will relish it or I will suffer it for only a brief time.

本句是由no matter引导的让步状语从句；no matter what (who/when etc.)...分别表示"无论何事""无论何人""无论何时"等，这个从句可以置主句之前，也可以置主句之后。由no matter + what等引导的让步状语从句。No matter后面接关系代词或关系副词引导状语从句在句中做让步状语。

例 No matter what you do, you must be very careful.
不管做什么事，你都必须非常细心。

No matter who you are (=Whoever you are), I'll never let you in.
无论你是谁，我绝不让你进去。

No matter which you choose, you will be satisfied.
不论你选择哪一个，你都会满意的。

③ Whenever I am struck down, in the future, by any terrible defeat, I will inquire of myself, after the first pain has passed, how I can turn that adversity into good.

本句中whenever引导时间状语从句；struck down表示"打倒、击落"。

例 Frank had been struck down by a massive heart attack.
弗兰克的身体已经被一场严重的心脏病拖垮了。

经典名句 Famous Classics

1. Never give up, never lose the opportunity to succeed.
不放弃就有成功的机会。

Seek the Seed of Triumph in Everyday Adversity
梅花香自苦寒来

2. Achievement provides the only real pleasure in life.
   有所成就是人生唯一的真正乐趣。

3. Man struggles upwards; water flows downwards.
   人往高处走，水往低处流。

4. Nothing seek, nothing find.
   无所求则无所获。

5. Progress is the activity of today and the assurance of tomorrow.
   进步乃今日之努力，明日之保证。

6. If you would go up high, then use your own legs! Do not let yourselves carried aloft; do not seat yourselves on other people's backs and heads.
   如果你想走到高处，就要使用自己的两条腿！不要让别人把你抬到高处；不要在别人的背上和头上。

7. To be without some of the things you want is an indispensable part of happiness.
   你追求不到的东西有时也是幸福不可缺少的一部分。

8. The greatest of faults is to be conscious of none.
   最严重的错误莫过于不觉得自己有任何错误。

读书笔记

29 The Answer Is Right There Above You
希望就在前方

If you put a **buzzard** in a pen six to eight feet square and entirely open at the top, the bird, in spite of its ability to fly, will be an absolute prisoner. The reason is that a buzzard always begins a flight from the ground with a run of ten to twelve feet. Without space to run, as is its habit, it will not even attempt to fly, but remain a **prisoner** for life in a small **jail** with no top.

The ordinary bat that flies around at night, who is a **remarkable nimble** creature in the air, cannot take off from a level place. If it is placed on the floor or flat ground, all it can do is to **shuffle** about helplessly and, no doubt, painfully, until it reaches some slight **elevation** from which it can throw itself into the air. Then, at once, it takes off like a flash.

A **bumblebee**, if dropped into an open **tumbler**, will be there until it dies, unless it is taken out. It never sees the means of escape at the top, but persists in trying to find some way out through the sides near the bottom. It will seek a way where none exists, until it completely destroys itself.

Many times in our lives, we are

如果你把一只秃鹫放在一个六到八英尺的围栏里，顶部完全打开，那只鸟尽管会飞，但绝对是个囚犯。原因是秃鹫从地面起飞前总要先助跑10～12英尺的距离，如果没有助跑空间，根据秃鹫的习性，它甚至不会去尝试飞行，依然停留在没有顶部的囚笼里面。

晚上飞来飞去的普通的蝙蝠，本是一种在空中极其敏捷的动物，但却无法在平地上起飞。如果你把它放在地板上或者水平地面上，那么它只能无助地摇摆，毫无疑问，它需要非常费力去找到一个高点，从而确保可以将自己抛入空中继续飞行。然后，它立即起飞，就像一道闪光。

如果一只大黄蜂掉进一个敞口的玻璃杯里，除非它被取出，否则它会一直待在那里。它永远不知道可以从杯口逃出，只坚持试图从杯底的四壁寻找出路。它将寻找一个不存在的出口，直到岁月彻底摧毁自己。

在生活中，很多时候我们被自己制定的决策和身边的

The Answer Is Right There Above You 希望就在前方

dropped, crumpled, and ground into the dirt by the decisions we make and the **circumstances** that come our way. But no matter what happened or what will happen, we should never lose our value and hope, remember to look up and hope may be right there above us. Sometimes, in many ways, there are lots of people like the buzzard, the bat and the bumblebee. They are struggling about with all their problems and frustrations, not realizing that the answer is right there above them.

环境所抛弃、踩踏，甚至碾入尘土。但是无论发生什么事或将要发生什么，我们都不应该失去自我价值和希望，记得抬头看看，或许希望就在我们上面。有时，在很多方面，有很多人就像秃鹫、蝙蝠和大黄蜂一样，他们努力解决他们所遇到的问题和挫折，并没有意识到答案就在前后。

单词解析 Word Analysis

buzzard ['bʌzəd] *n.* 秃鹫

例 The buzzard would have gotten fat on us all right.
秃鹫光吃我们就吃饱了。

prisoner ['prɪznə(r)] *n.* 囚犯；犯人；俘虏；刑事被告

例 The committee is concerned about the large number of prisoners sharing cells.
这个委员会对牢房拥挤问题表示担忧。

jail [dʒeɪl] *n.* 监狱；拘留所

例 Three prisoners escaped from a jail.
3名囚犯越狱了。

remarkable [rɪ'mɑːkəbl] *adj.* 显著的；卓越的；异常的，引人注目的

例 It is quite remarkable that doctors have been so wrong about this.
医生们对此有过如此错误的认识真是很不寻常。

nimble ['nɪmbl] *adj.* 灵活的；敏捷的；机敏的

例 Everything had been stitched by Molly's nimble fingers.
每一件东西都是莫莉灵巧的双手缝制出来的。

shuffle ['ʃʌfl] *vi.* 洗牌；曳脚而行；搬移；搁置；随手放

例 Moira shuffled across the kitchen.
莫伊拉拖着脚穿过厨房。

elevation [ˌelɪ'veɪʃn] *n.* 高处，高地，高度，海拔

例 We're probably at an elevation of about 13,000 feet above sea level.
我们可能在大约海拔13000英尺的高度。

bumblebee ['bʌmblbiː] *n.* <动>大黄蜂，雄蜂

例 The bumblebee sizzed right under his straw hat.
大黄蜂就在他的草帽底下丝丝作声。

tumbler ['tʌmblə(r)] *n.* 平底玻璃杯

例 He took a tumbler from a cupboard.
他从碗橱里拿出一只平底玻璃杯。

语法知识点 *Grammar Points*

① **If you put a buzzard in a pen six to eight feet square and entirely open at the top, the bird, in spite of its ability to fly, will be an absolute prisoner.**

本句是由 if 引导的条件状语从句；句中 in spite of 为固定短语，表示"虽然，尽管……"。

例 In spite of great peril, I have survived.
虽然处境非常危险，我还是挺过来了。

② **The reason is that a buzzard always begins a flight from the ground with a run of ten to twelve feet.**

本句是由 that 引导的表语从句，此处 that 不可省略。that 可以省略的情况主要应用于宾语从句或者先行词在从句中充当宾语的定语从句。

例如：宾语从句：I promise that I will study hard. 这里的that可以省略。
定语从句：This is the factory that we visited yesterday. 这里的that可以省略。

③ **The ordinary bat that flies around at night, who is a remarkable nimble creature in the air, cannot take off from a level place.**

本句中 that 引导定语从句，先行词 the ordinary bat 在从句中做主语，不能省略；who 同样引导定语从句，先行词为 the ordinary bat，整句主干为 The ordinary bat...cannot...。

fly around 表示"飞来飞去，急匆匆地走"；take off 表示"起飞"。

例 What I find the most disgusting is when a cockroach fly around the room.
我发现最恶心的是有蟑螂在房间里面飞。

We eventually took off at 11 o'clock and arrived in Venice at 1:30.
我们终于在11点起飞，1:30到达威尼斯。

④ **It never sees the means of escape at the top, but persists in trying to find some way out through the sides near the bottom.**

本句中 persist in doing 表示"坚持；固执于"；find way out 表示"找到出路"。

例 If you persist in misbehaving, you'll be punished.
如果你坚持胡作非为，就将受到惩罚。

We try to find a way out of our dilemma.
我们试图摆脱困境。

经典名句 Famous Classics

1. A man has choice to begin love, but not to end it.
一个人开始去爱上谁的时候，他可以有所选择，但当他要结束爱情的时候，他可没有选择了。

2. The reason why a great man is great is that he resolves to be a great man.
伟人之所以伟大，是因为他立志要成为伟大的人。

3. Logic will get you from A to B. Imagination will take you everywhere.
   逻辑会带你从A点到达B点，想象力将把你带到任何地方。

4. The greatest test of courage on earth is to bear defeat without losing heart.
   世界上对勇气的最大考验是忍受失败而不丧失信心。

5. The best preparation for tomorrow is doing your best today.
   对明天做好的准备就是今天做到最好！

6. Living without an aim is like sailing without a compass.
   生活没有目标，犹如航海没有罗盘。

7. Live beautifully, dream passionately, love completely.
   活要活得美好，梦要梦得热烈，爱要爱得完整。

读书笔记

30 Dark Clouds Always in the Past
乌云总会过去

While my friends attended their universities in great delight, I restarted my senior high school life. My spirit sank at the **prospect** of starting all over again. Surrounded by strange classmates, I felt like I was in a **maze** and was sorry for myself. There were some **complex** feelings in my mind. I was frightened, nervous and lonely.

To make matters worse, I recalled my failure again and again, which put more pressure on me than I could bear. As a result, I was always feeling down during class.

My teacher found me **spiritless**. One day he asked me to come to his office and told me about his attitude towards life: we might suffer from making mistakes, but it's important to model ourselves into the people we will become. All the growing pains and the embarrassing things we may experience are part of the process. We never stop growing up, so learn from it and keep up your spirit! At last, he added if you are optimistic, things you want may happen to you!

Warm feelings rush through my

当我的朋友们高兴地去上大学的时候，我重新开始了我的高中生活。我的精神沉浸在全部重新开始的期待中。被陌生的同学包围着，我觉得自己在迷宫里，为自己感到难过。我心里有些复杂的感觉。我感到害怕、紧张和孤独。

更糟糕的是，我不断地回想起我的失败，压力几乎大到我无法忍受的地步。结果，上课时我总是情绪低落。

我的老师发现我无精打采。有一天，他让我到他的办公室，告诉我他对生活的态度：我们可能会犯错误，但重要的是把自己塑造成我们将成为的人。我们经历的所有成长的痛苦和尴尬的事情都是这个过程的一部分。我们永远不会停止成长，所以从中吸取教训，保持你的精神！最后，他补充说，如果你保持乐观心态，你想要的事情可能会发生在你身上！

温暖的感觉掠过我的灵魂，当我走出办公室的刹那，我发现我的世界突然光明了。

soul. I suddenly found the sun shining again when I stepped out of his office.

With the teacher's help, I eventually got over my **depression**. From then on, I no longer bowed my head but began smiling to my classmates. I would put up my hand confidently in class and kid with my new friends in my spare time. **Meanwhile**, I was gradually embraced by my classmates.

Now faced with **fierce** competition, we all study **strenuously**, and every second counts. However, there is an atmosphere of mutual trust and respect between us. I love my class; I love my classmates!

To be **frank**, I still have a thirst for my dream university, but I'm not afraid of the failure because I can profit by it.

With parents and teachers great expectation, I'm quite certain of my future and I'm sure I can fly high.

在老师的帮助下我终于从低落中走出来。从那以后，我再也不垂头丧气，而是微笑面对同学。我会在上课时自信举手回答问题并且在课余时间和新的朋友一起开玩笑。与此同时，我逐渐被同学们接纳。

面对激烈的竞争，我们都在努力学习，每一秒都很重要。然而，我们之间有一种相互信任和尊重的气氛。我爱我的班级，我爱我的同学！

坦率地说，我仍然渴望我的梦想大学，但我不害怕失败，因为我依然可以受益良多。

有了父母和老师的厚望，我对我的未来充满信心，我相信我能飞得很高。

单词解析 Word Analysis

prospect ['prɒspekt] *n.* 前景；期望；眺望处；景象

例 Unfortunately, there is little prospect of seeing these big questions answered.
不幸的是，几乎不可能看到这些重大问题得到回复。

maze [meɪz] *n.* 迷宫；迷惑；错综复杂；迷宫图

例 The palace has extensive gardens, a maze, and tennis courts.
这座宫殿有几座大花园、一处迷宫和几个网球场。

Dark Clouds Always in the Past
乌云总会过去

complex ['kɒmpleks] *adj.* 复杂的；难懂的；复合的
- 例 The various systems are coupled together in complex arrays.
  多个系统在复杂的数组中连接起来。

spiritless ['spɪrɪtləs] *adj.* 死气沉沉；无精打采的；蔫；打不起精神来
- 例 They were too spiritless even to resist.
  他们无精打采的，甚至都没有抵抗。

depression [dɪ'preʃn] *n.* 萎靡不振，沮丧
- 例 Mr. Thomas was suffering from depression.
  托马斯先生患有抑郁症。

meanwhile ['miːnwaɪl] *adv.* 同时，其间
- 例 Brush the aborigines with oil, add salt and pepper, and bake till soft. Meanwhile, heat the remaining oil in a heavy pan.
  把油涂在茄子上，加盐和胡椒烤至松软。与此同时，在厚锅中加热剩余的油。

fierce [fɪəs] *adj.* 猛烈的；凶猛的，残忍的；狂热的
- 例 They look like the teeth of some fierce animal.
  它们看上去像某种猛兽的牙齿。

strenuously ['strenjʊəslɪ] *adv.* 奋发地，费力地，勤奋地
- 例 He strenuously denies all the allegations against him.
  他据理力争地否定了所有对他的控告。

frank [fræŋk] *adj.* 坦白的，直率的；清楚表明的；明显的
- 例 To be frank, he could also be a bit of a bore.
  老实说，他有时也会让人厌烦。

语法知识点 Grammar Points

① **Surrounded by strange classmates, I felt like I was in a maze and was sorry for myself.**

本句是伴随状语从句，当前后主语一致时，主语和be动词要一起省略，完整句式应该为 I was surrounded by...。

be surrounded by 表示"被……包围"; be sorry for 表示"为……感到难过,歉疚"。

> Is it important for you to be surrounded by color?
> 被色彩包围对你来说很重要吗?
> You'll be sorry for what you said sooner or later.
> 你早晚会为你所说的后悔。

② To make matters worse, I recalled my failure again and again, which put more pressure on me than I could bear.

本句是由 which 引导的非限定性定语从句,此处不能用 that 替代;to make matters worse 为固定搭配,表示"更糟糕的是";again and again 表示"再三地,反复地";put pressure on 表示"强迫,促使;要挟"。

> I lost my way in the forest, and to make matters worse, it became dark.
> 我在森林里迷了路。更糟糕的是,天开始黑了。
> She felt and looked at the cloth again and again and praised it.
> 她把布摸了又摸,看了又看,说这布不错。
> He may have put pressure on her to agree.
> 他可能向她施加了压力,迫使她同意。

③ With the teacher's help, I eventually got over my depression. From then on, I no longer bowed my head but began smiling to my classmates.

本句中 with 引导独立主格结构;from then on 表示"从此;从那时起";bow one's head 表示"低头;俯首"。

> The kid feels excited with so many places of interest to visit.
> 有这么多的名胜可参观,小孩很激动。
> From then on, they were taking no chances.
> 从那时起,他们就不再冒险了。
> On this day it is traditional to bow one's head and give thanks for life's many blessings.
> 在这一天,人们按传统应该低头感谢生活中的幸事。

本句中同样涉及 begin 的用法,一般而言,begin to do sth. 是开始打算要做某事,是指事情还未做,准备开始做;begin doing sth 是指开始做某事,表示动作正在进行。

Dark Clouds Always in the Past
乌云总会过去 30

> Only after he left school did he begin to do chimp research.
> 直到他离开学校后,他才开始对黑猩猩进行研究。
>
> That which you plan to participate in or contribute to post stasis you can begin doing now.
> 你们所计划参与或贡献去促成停滞期的行动,现在可以开始了。

④ Meanwhile, I was gradually embraced by my classmates.

Meanwhile 表示"与此同时";be embraced by 表示"被接受,被包含,被拥抱"。

> Offerings deliver real value to the customer, and are more likely to be embraced by developers.
> 产品为客户带来了真正的价值,更可能被开发人员接受。

⑤ To be frank, I still have a thirst for my dream university, but I'm not afraid of the failure because I can profit by it.

本句中 because 引导原因状语从句;to be frank 表示"坦率地说;老实说;说实话";be afraid of 表示"害怕,担忧"。

> To be frank with you, Harvey, I may have made a mistake.
> 老实跟你讲,哈维,我可能犯了个错。
>
> Why should a great community like a university be afraid of nihilism?
> 为什么像大学这样人才济济的社区要害怕虚无主义呢?

经典名句 Famous Classics

1. Time is a bird for ever on the wing.
   时间是一只永远在飞翔的鸟。

2. It never will rain roses when we want to have more roses, we must plant trees.
   天上不会掉下玫瑰来,如果想要更多的玫瑰,必须自己种植。

3. If you have great talents, industry will improve them; if you have but moderate abilities, industry will supply their deficiency.
   如果你很有天赋,勤勉会使其更加完善;如果你能力一般,勤勉会补足其缺陷。

4. Until you make peace with who you are, you'll never be content with what you have.
   除非你能和真实的自己和平相处，否则你永远不会对已拥有的东西感到满足。

5. If you would go up high, then use your own legs! Do not let yourselves carried aloft; do not seat yourselves on other people's backs and heads.
   如果你想走到高处，就要使用自己的两条腿！不要让别人把你抬到高处；不要坐在别人的背上和头上。

6. Do not know how high the sky is until one climbs up the tops of mountains, and do not know how thick the earth is until one comes to the deep river.
   不登高山，不知天之高也；不临深溪，不知地之厚也。

7. The reasonable man adapts himself to the world; the unreasonable one persists in trying to adapt the world to himself.
   明白事理的人使自己适应世界；不明事理的人想使世界适应自己。

读书笔记

31 Never Give Up
永不放弃

When he stepped off the plane in Washington D.C, following the 1992 Winter Games, and everyone in the **terminal** started clapping. Paul Wylie almost stopped in his tracks. Who's behind me? He wondered. Despite the silver medal in his pocket, he couldn't believe that the applause was for him. From that moment on, Paul recognized that his life would never be the same.

The silver medal he earned in Albertville, France, **ushered** the 27-year-old figure skater into a new existence. He was no longer a nobody who choked at big events, like the 1988 Calgary Olympics, where he finished an unimpressive 10th. No longer the **recipient** of advice from judges who, after Paul's performance in the 91 World Championships, suggested that he quit: "Make room for the younger skaters."

No longer the target of loaded questions from reporters covering the 91 Olympic Trials. No longer the skater incapable of finishing ahead of U.S. National Champion Todd Eldredge or three-time defending World Champion Kurt Browning of Canada. Now Paul

1992年冬奥会闭幕后，保罗·怀利抵达华盛顿。走下飞机时，欢迎的人群开始鼓掌。他差点停下了脚步。谁在后面呀？他心里嘀咕。虽说有银牌在囊中，他怎么也不敢相信这掌声是献给他的。从那一刻起，保罗意识到自己的生活从此永远地改变了。

这位27岁的花样滑冰运动员在法国的阿尔贝维尔获得了银牌，从此走向全新的生活。1988年的卡尔加里冬奥会上，他表现平平，只得了第10名，可如今他再也不是在大型赛事中举止失措的无名小卒了；1991年的世界锦标赛上，保罗比赛结束后，裁判建议他退出冰坛，"给年轻选手让位"，如今再也听不到这样的建议了。

跟踪报道1991年冬奥会选拔赛的记者们曾问他"你来这儿干什么？"，如今再也不会有这种别有用心的提问了。他再也不是美国冠军托德·埃尔德雷奇的手下败将，再也不会被三度问鼎世界冠军宝座的加拿大运动员库尔特·布朗宁

Wylie was an Olympic hero. He was an **athlete** who kept going when doubters suggested he quit. He was a recent Harvard University graduate who had frequently fantasized about life without **grueling** hours on the ice, but who persevered anyway. He was a young man who had discovered and demonstrated that goals can be reached no matter how many obstacles and botched attempts lie in the way.

Paul says, "It wasn't until I stepped off the plane that I realized people considered me a hero. They were changed by my story. They were changed by the fact that I was able to persevere and win the silver medal even though almost everyone had counted me out."

At times, Paul had almost counted himself out. Things definitely changed in 1992 in Albertville. With medal in hand, Paul was suddenly ushered into a world of **lucrative endorsements** and **figure-skating** world tours of exclusive events and autograph seekers. Everything you might expect of a **celebrity** hero, but none of what Paul himself believes merits the honor of that title.

As an Olympic medal loses its **luster** after years of storage, a hero will lose his **credibility** if he stops looking to the needs of others. When Paul joins

甩在身后。现在保罗·怀利成了奥运英雄。虽然有些人对他没有信心，建议他放弃，可他仍然勇往直前。虽然这个刚出校门的哈佛毕业生经常幻想离开严酷的冰上训练生活会是怎样，但依然苦苦坚持着。这个年轻人发现：不管途中有多少障碍，要经历多少次失败，目标终能实现，而且他证明了这一点。

保罗说："走下飞机，我才意识到人们把我当成了英雄。他们对我的看法改变了，因为我获胜了。他们的看法改变了，因为我坚持不懈并且得了银牌，虽然没什么人看好我。"

有时，保罗也几乎不看好自己了。1992年在阿尔贝维尔，事情完全改观了。手中拿着奖牌，保罗突然进入到一个全新的世界：不断的签约、花样滑冰巡回赛、独家采访、追星族要求签名。总之，凡是一个声名鹊起的英雄能得到的一切他都得到了，但保罗认为这一头衔值得称道的东西远不在此。

收藏多年之后，奥运奖牌会退去它最初的光泽；若是不再关注别人的需要，英雄也会失去其知名度。和成千上万的人们一同观看盐湖城冬奥会时，保罗很清楚，每个胜利的背后，每次

Never Give Up
永不放弃

the thousands of others watching the Olympics in Salt Lake City, he knows that behind the scenes of each victory, of each record-setting finish, stand countless stories of everyday heroes. Heroes who refuse to give up.

打破纪录的背后，都有无数日日坚持不懈英雄的故事，那种永不放弃的英雄故事。

单词解析 Word Analysis

terminal ['tɜːmɪnl] *n.* 终端；终点站；航空站

例 My own house feels as filthy and chaotic as a bus terminal.
我家的房子感觉又脏又乱，活像公共汽车终点站。

usher ['ʌʃə(r)] *v.* 引领，招待；做招待员；宣告

例 I ushered him into the office.
我领他去办公室。

recipient [rɪ'sɪpiənt] *n.* 接受者；容器；容纳者

例 A suppressed immune system puts a transplant recipient at risk of other infections.
接受器官移植的病人免疫系统受到抑制后很可能会感染其他疾病。

athlete ['æθliːt] *n.* 运动员；体育家；强壮的人

例 Daley Thompson was a great athlete.
戴利·汤普森是位著名的运动员。

grueling ['gruəlɪŋ] *adj.* 紧张的，激烈的，使极度疲劳的

例 We got home after a grueling drive.
经过一段令人精疲力竭的开车我们到家了。

lucrative ['luːkrətɪv] *adj.* 获利多的，赚钱的；合算的

例 Thousands of ex-army officers have found lucrative jobs in private security firms.
数以千计的退伍军官在私营保安公司找到了收入不菲的工作。

endorsements [enˈdɔːsmənts] *n.* 签约，赞同

例 He racked up endorsements from newspapers, unions and chambers of commerce.
他从报纸、工会和商会那里得到了很多的支持。

figure-skating [ˈfɪɡə ˈskeɪtɪŋ] *n.* 花样滑冰

例 I have particular interest in watching the matches of diving, figure skating and swimming.
我特别喜欢看跳水、花样滑冰和游泳比赛。

celebrity [səˈlebrəti] *n.* 名流；名声；名人，知名人士；名誉

例 In 1944, at the age of 30, Hersey suddenly became a celebrity.
1944年，30岁的赫西一夜成名。

luster [ˈlʌstə] *n.* 光泽；光彩；光辉；荣耀

例 These products have crystal luster and strong vision effect.
这些产品有水晶光泽和强大的视觉效果。

语法知识点 Grammar Points

① **Paul Wylie almost stopped in his tracks.**

本句中固定短语 stop in one's tracks 表示"突然停下"。

例 The criminal stopped in his tracks when he heard the footsteps behind him.
当罪犯听到他身后的脚步声时，他突然停了下来。

② **Despite the silver medal in his pocket, he couldn't believe that the applause was for him.**

本句中despite引导让步状语从句，介词表示"即使，尽管"之意；同时despite 还可做名词，表示"侮辱；憎恨；怨恨"。

例 Despite a thorough investigation, no trace of Dr. Southwell has been found.
尽管进行了彻底的调查，还是没有发现索思韦尔博士的任何踪迹。

that 在句中引导宾语从句，believe 后接that 引导宾语从句时，无论否定主句还是从句，否定都要提前。

Never Give Up
永不放弃 31

> 例　I don't believe that George ever had to punish the children.
> 我认为乔治根本没有必要处罚孩子们。

③ **He was an athlete who kept going when doubters suggested he quit.**

本句中 who 引导定语从句，先行词 an athlete；后面 when 引导时间状语从句，表示"当……时候"。

> 例　You can chat to other people who are online.
> 你可以和其他在线的人聊天。
>
> When I met the Gills, I had been gardening for nearly ten years.
> 遇到吉尔一家时我已经做了近10年的园艺工作。

④ **It wasn't until I stepped off the plane that I realized people considered me a hero.**

本句为强调句型 It is / was not until...+从句，强调部分为 I stepped off the plane。

> 例　It was not until I finish my homework that I was admit to play computer games.
> 直到完成我的作业我才被允许玩游戏。

⑤ **At times, Paul had almost counted himself out.**

本句中 counted...out 表示"把……排除在外"；at times 表示"有时；间或"。

> 例　The match took nearly three hours and was interrupted at times by rain.
> 比赛进行了将近3个小时，几次因雨而暂停。
>
> If you're going swimming tomorrow morning, you can count me out, because I'll be preparing for an examination.
> 如果你们明天早晨去游泳，就把我排除在外吧，因为我要准备考试。

经典名句 Famous Classics

1. Never give up, never lose the opportunity to succeed.
不放弃就有成功的机会。

173

2. Don't try so hard, the best things come when you least expect them to.
不要着急,最好的总会在最不经意的时候出现。

3. I disapprove of what you say, but I will defend to the death your right to say it.
我不同意你说的话,但我愿意誓死捍卫你说话的权利。

4. Twenty years from now you will be more disappointed by the things that you didn't do than by the things you did.
今后二十年你会因为没做某事,而不是做了某事而失望。

5. It is not enough to be industrious, so are the ants. What are you industrious about?
光勤劳是不够的,蚂蚁也是勤劳的。要看你为什么而勤劳。

6. Hope for the best, prepare for the worst.
抱最好的希望,做最坏的打算。

读书笔记

32 Hard Life
艰辛的人生

A life of **slothful** ease, a life of that peace which springs **merely** from lack either of desire or of power to strive after great things, is as little worthy of a nation as an individual.

We do not admire the man of **timid** peace. We admire the man who embodies **victorious** efforts, the man who never wrongs his neighbor, who is prompt to help a friend, but who has those virile qualities necessary to win in the **stern strife** of actual life. It is hard to fail, but it is worse never to have tried to succeed. In this life we get nothing save by effort. Freedom from effort in the present merely means that there has been effort stored up in the past. A man can be freed from the necessity of work only by the fact that he or his fathers before him have worked to good purpose. If the freedom thus purchased is used aright, and the man still does actual work, though of a different kind, whether as a writer or a general, whether in the field of politics or in the field of **exploration** and adventure, he shows he deserves his good **fortune**.

But if he treats this period of

一种怠惰安逸的生活，一种仅仅是由于缺少追寻伟大事物的渴望或能力而导致的悠闲生活，这对国家与个人都是毫无价值的。

我们不欣赏那种怯懦安逸的人。我们钦佩那种奋力向上的人，那种永不屈待邻人，能随时帮助朋友，但是也具有那些刚健的品质，足以在现实生活的严酷斗争中获取胜利的人。失败是难以忍受的，但更为糟糕的是从来不去努力争取成功。在人的这一生中，任何的收获都要通过努力去得到。现在不做任何的努力，只不过意味着在过去有过努力的积蓄。一个人不必工作，除非他或其先辈们曾经努力工作过，并取得了丰厚的收获。假如他能够把获得的这种自由加以正确地运用，仍然做些实际的工作，尽管那些工作是属于另一类的，不论是做一名作家还是将军，不论是在政界还是在探险和冒险方面做些事情，都表明了他没有辜负自己的好运。

但是，假如他未将这段需要从事实际工作的自由时期

freedom from the need of actual labor as a period, not of preparation, but of mere enjoyment, even though perhaps not of vicious enjoyment, he shows that he is simply a cumberer on the earth's surface; and he surely unfits himself to hold his own place with his fellows, if the need to do so should again arise. A mere life of ease is not in the end a very satisfactory life, and, above all, it is a life which ultimately unfits those who follow it for serious work in the world.

As it is with the individual, so it is with the nation. It is a base **untruth** to say that happy is the nation that has no history. Thrice happy is the nation that has a **glorious** history. Far better it is to dare mighty things, to win glorious triumphs, even though checkered by failure, than to take rank with those poor spirits who neither enjoy much nor suffer much, because they live in the gray **twilight** that knows neither victory nor defeat.

用于准备，而仅仅是用于享乐（即使他所从事的或许并非不良的享乐），那也就表明了他只是地球表面上的一个赘疣；而且如果那种需要再度出现的话，他肯定无法在同僚之中维持自己的地位。一种纯粹安逸的生活终究并不是一种令人很满意的生活，而且，最主要的是，过那种生活的人最终肯定没有能力担当起世上之重任。

对于个人是如此，对于国家也是这样。有人说一个没有历史的国家是得天独厚的，这是根本错误的。一种得天独厚的优越感来源于一个国家所具有的光荣历史。敢于挑战非比寻常的事物，去赢得光辉的胜利，即使其中掺杂着失败，那也远胜于那些既没有享受多大快乐也没有遭受多大痛苦的平庸之辈，因为他们生活在一个既享受不到胜利也不会遇到挫败的灰暗的境界中。

单词解析 Word Analysis

slothful [ˈsləʊθfl] *adj.* 懒惰的，懒散的，不活跃的

例 He was not slothful: he had been busy all night.
他可不懒，昨晚他忙了整整一夜。

Hard Life 艰辛的人生 32

merely ['mɪəli] *adv.* 只是；仅仅，只不过
例 Michael is now merely a good friend.
迈克尔现在仅仅是个不错的朋友而已。

timid ['tɪmɪd] *adj.* 胆小的；羞怯的
例 As a timid child, Isabella had learned obedience at an early age.
伊莎贝拉是一个羞怯的孩子，很小就学会了顺从。

victorious [vɪk'tɔːriəs] *adj.* 胜利的；得胜的
例 In 1978 he played for the victorious Argentinian side in the World Cup.
1978年，他效力于获得世界杯冠军的阿根廷队。

stern [stɜːn] *adj.* 严肃的；严厉的
例 Mr. Straw issued a stern warning to those who persist in violence.
斯特劳先生向那些坚持进行暴力活动的人发出了严正警告。

strife [straɪf] *n.* 冲突；斗争；争吵
例 Money is a major cause of strife in many marriages.
金钱是很多婚姻不和的一个主要原因。

exploration [ˌekspləˈreɪʃn] *n.* 探测，勘探，探险
例 A big program of oil exploration has begun offshore.
一个大规模的石油勘探计划正在近海展开。

fortune ['fɔːtʃuːn] *n.* 幸运；（某人的）命运
例 We had to eat out all the time. It ended up costing a fortune.
我们不得不总在外面吃饭，结果花了很多钱。

untruth [ˌʌnˈtruːθ] *n.* 谎言；不真实，虚假
例 The Advertising Standards Authority accused estate agents of using blatant untruths.
广告标准管理局控告房地产代理商使用无耻的谎言。

glorious ['glɔːriəs] *adj.* 辉煌的；荣誉的
例 She had missed the glorious blooms of the Mediterranean spring.
她错过了地中海春季鲜花怒放的绚丽美景。

twilight ['twaɪlaɪt] *n.* 黎明，黄昏，暮光

例 They returned at twilight, and set off for one of the promenade bars.
他们黄昏时分回来，然后去了一家步行街酒吧。

语法知识点 *Grammar Points*

① **A life of slothful ease, a life of that peace which springs merely from lack either of desire or of power to strive after great things, is as little worthy of a nation as an individual.**

本句是由which引导的定语从句，句中either...or...表示"要么……要么……"。

例 He must be either mad or drunk.
他要么是疯了，要么是喝醉了。

strive after 表示"奋斗，争取"。

例 Some people continually strive after perfection, even though they know it's impossible to reach.
有些人执着地追求完美，尽管他们也知道那是不可能的。

as...as... 表示"与……一样"。

例 This new transformation is at least as consequential as that one was
这一新的转变至少和那次一样重要。

② **We admire the man who embodies victorious efforts, the man who never wrongs his neighbor, who is prompt to help a friend, but who has those virile qualities necessary to win in the stern strife of actual life.**

本句中存在多个定语从句，都由who引导，先行词为the man，先行词在从句中做主语。当who引导定语从句时要注意以下几点：
1）who引导的定语从句的先行词是表示人的名词或代词。

例 The student who is answering the question is John.
正在回答问题的那个学生是约翰。

2）who是主格，在定语从句中做主语，此时不能省略。

Hard Life
艰辛的人生

例 The person who was here yesterday is a musician.
昨天来这儿的那个人是位音乐家。

3）在定语从句中，who在人称、数上和其前面的先行词保持一致。

例 Do you know the boy who is standing over there?
你认识站在那边的那个男孩吗？

4）若先行词中既有人又有物，关系代词用that而不用who。

例 He watched the children and boxes that filled the car.
他看见了塞满汽车的孩子和箱子。

5）若先行词前面有形容词最高级、序数词修饰，关系代词用that而不用who。

例 Yao Ming is the best basketball player that I know.
姚明是我知道的最好的篮球运动员。

③ **A mere life of ease is not in the end a very satisfactory life, and, above all, it is a life which ultimately unfits those who follow it for serious work in the world.**

本句中which引导定语从句，先行词是a life；who引导定语从句，先行词是those。

above all 表示"首要的是，尤其；最重要的是"。

例 In this matter we must place the common cause above all else.
在这件事情上，我们必须把共同事业放在高于一切的位置上。

④ **It is a base untruth to say that happy is the nation that has no history.**

本句中it is a base untruth to say that...为特殊句式，表示"那样说是不真实的"，该搭配应用广泛，it 做形式主语，to say that...为真正主语；第二个that引导定语从句。

例 So it is hard to say that learning English is easy, because a good command of English depends upon a lot of practice.
所以很难说学英语是件轻而易举的事情。因为，要想掌握好英语，就得做大量的练习。

经典名句 Famous Classics

1. While there is life there is hope.
   一息若存,希望不灭。

2. Never underestimate your power to change yourself!
   永远不要低估你改变自我的能力!

3. It is easier to fight for principles than to live up to them.
   为原则而斗争比实践该原则要容易。

4. I can make it through the rain. I can stand up once again on my own.
   我可以穿越云雨,也可以东山再起。

5. When I was young, I admired clever people. Now that I am old, I admire kind people.
   少时喜欢聪明人,老来喜欢仁厚人。

6. Work is the grand cure of all the maladies and miseries that ever beset mankind.
   工作是医治人间一切病痛和疾苦的万应良药。

7. We must accept finite disappointment, but we must never lose infinite hope.
   我们必须接受失望,因为它是有限的,但千万不可失去希望,因为它是无穷的。

读书笔记

33 If I Rest, I Rust
如果我休息，我就会生锈

The **significant inscription** found on an old key—"If I rest, I rust"—would be an excellent **motto** for those who are afflicted with the slightest bit of **idleness**. Even the most **industrious** person might adopt it with advantage to serve as a reminder. If one allows his **faculties** to rest, like the iron in the unused key, they will soon show signs of rust. And ultimately, they cannot do the work required of them.

Those who would attain the heights reached and kept by great men must keep their faculties polished by **constant** use, so that they may unlock the doors of knowledge, the gate that guard the entrances to the professions, to science, art, literature, agriculture, every department of human **endeavor**.

Industry keeps bright the key that opens the treasury of achievement. If Hugh Miller, after toiling all day in a quarry, had devoted his evenings to rest and recreation, he would never have become a famous geologist. The celebrated **mathematician**, Edmund Stone, would never have published a mathematical dictionary, never have

在一把旧钥匙上发现了一则意义深远的铭文——如果我休息，我就会生锈。对于那些懒散而烦恼的人来说，这将是至理名言。甚至最为勤勉的人也以此作为警示：如果一个人有才能而不用，就像废弃钥匙上的铁一样，这些才能很快就会生锈，并最终无法完成安排给自己的工作。

有些人想取得伟人所获得并保持的成就，他们就必须不断运用自身才能，以便开启知识的大门，即那些通往人类努力探求的各个领域的大门，这些领域包括各种职业：科学、艺术、文学、农业等。

勤奋使开启成功宝库的钥匙保持光亮。如果休·米勒在采石场劳作一天后，晚上的时光用来休息消遣的话，他就不会成为名垂青史的地质学家。著名数学家爱德蒙·斯通如果闲暇时无所事事，就不会出版数学词典，也不会发现开启数学之门的钥匙。如果苏格兰青年弗格森在山坡上放羊时，让他那思维活跃的大脑处于休息

found the key to science of mathematics, if he had given his spare moments to idleness. Had the little Scotch lad, Ferguson, allowed the busy brain to go to sleep while he tended sheep on the hillside instead of calculating the position of the stars by a string of beads, he would never have become a famous astronomer.

Labor vanquishes all—not **inconstant**, **spasmodic**, or ill-directed labor; but faithful, **unremitting**, daily effort toward a well-directed purpose. Just as truly as eternal vigilance is the price of liberty, so is eternal industry the price of noble and enduring success.

状态，而不是借助一串珠子计算星星的位置，他就不会成为著名的天文学家。

劳动征服一切。这里所指的劳动不是断断续续的、间歇性的或方向偏差的劳动，而是坚定的、不懈的、方向正确的每日劳动。正如要想拥有自由就要时刻保持警惕一样，要想取得伟大的、持久的成功，就必须坚持不懈地努力。

单词解析 *Word Analysis*

significant [sɪɡˈnɪfɪkənt] *adj.* 重要的；有意义的

例 A small but significant number of 11-year-olds are illiterate.
数量不多但仍有相当一部分11岁孩子是文盲。

inscription [ɪnˈskrɪpʃn] *n.* （作者）题词；献词

例 The inscription reads: "To Emma, with love from Harry".
题赠写着："献给爱玛，爱你的哈里。"

motto [ˈmɒtəʊ] *n.* 座右铭；格言；箴言

例 Our motto is "Plan for the worst and hope for the best".
我们的格言是"做最坏的打算，抱最大的希望"。

idleness [ˈaɪdlnəs] *n.* 懒惰；闲散

例 Luck and idleness gave me my first chance.
运气和懒惰给了我第一个机会。

If I Rest, I Rust
如果我休息，我就会生锈

industrious [ɪnˈdʌstriəs] *adj.* 勤劳的，勤奋的；勤恳的

例 Apart from his intelligence, he was tirelessly industrious.
除了很聪颖之外，他还是一个孜孜不倦的勤奋的人。

faculty [ˈfæklti] *n.* 能力，才能

例 It is also a myth that the faculty of hearing is greatly increased in blind people.
盲人的听力会大幅增强也是一种谬谈。

constant [ˈkɒnstənt] *adj.* 不断的，持续的

例 She suggests that women are under constant pressure to be abnormally thin.
她暗示说女性总是处在保持身材异常瘦削的压力之下。

endeavor [ɪnˈdevə] *n.* 努力，尽力

例 We made an earnest endeavor to persuade her.
我们郑重其事地努力说服她。

mathematician [ˌmæθəməˈtɪʃn] *n.* 数学家

例 The risks can be so complex that banks hire mathematicians to puzzle them out.
由于风险过高，银行便聘请数学家来解决这些问题。

inconstant [ɪnˈkɒnstənt] *adj.* （感情）易变的，无常的；常变的

例 But now, the gap is shrinking, and China's aniline market has become complicated and inconstant.
但是现在，这个差距正在缩小，而且中国的苯胺市场已经变得复杂多变。

spasmodic [spæzˈmɒdɪk] *adj.* 痉挛性；痉挛的

例 He managed to stifle the spasmodic sobs of panic rising in his throat.
他惊慌得差一点哭了起来，不过还是竭力地克制住了。

unremitting [ˌʌnrɪˈmɪtɪŋ] *adj.* 不懈的；坚持不懈

例 I was sent to boarding school, where I spent six years of unremitting misery.
我被送到寄宿学校呆了6年，期间我的生活一直很悲惨。

语法知识点 *Grammar Points*

① **Those who would attain the heights reached and kept by great men must keep their faculties polished by constant use, so that they may unlock the doors of knowledge, the gate that guard the entrances to the professions, to science, art, literature, agriculture, every department of human endeavor.**

本句较长，分析以 so that 为分界线，so that 在此句中引导目的状语从句；who 在句中引导定语从句。

② **Had the little Scotch lad, Ferguson, allowed the busy brain to go to sleep while he tended sheep on the hillside instead of calculating the position of the stars by a string of beads, he would never have become a famous astronomer.**

本句为部分倒装语序，属于以 had/were/should 开头省略 if 的虚拟条件句，句子的主干是 Had the little Scotch...allowed the busy brain..., he would never have become a famous astronomer. 相当于if the little Scotch...allowed the busy brain...he would never have become a famous astronomer.

例 Were they here now, they could help us. =If they were here now, they could help us.
要是他们在这儿的话，就会帮助我们了。
Should it rain, the crops would be saved. =Were it to rain, the crops would be saved.
假如下雨，庄稼就有救了。

③ **Just as truly as eternal vigilance is the price of liberty, so is eternal industry the price of noble and enduring success.**

本句中 just as ... so ... 是英语中的一种常见用法，表示"正如……一样；就像……一样"。

例 Just as French people enjoy their wine, so the British people enjoy their beer.
英国人喜欢啤酒就像法国人喜欢红酒一样。

经典名句 Famous Classics

1. If you do not learn to think when you are young, you may never learn.
   如果你年轻时不学会思考，那就永远不会。

2. There is only one success— to be able to spend your life in your own way.
   只有一种成功，那就是能够用自己的方式度过自己的一生。

3. Try not to become a man of success but rather try to become a man of value.
   不要为成功而努力，要为成为一个有价值的人而努力。

4. The failures and reverses which await men — and one after another sadden the brow of youth — add a dignity to the prospect of human life, which no Arcadian success would do.
   尽管失败和挫折等待着人们，一次次地夺走青春的容颜，但却给人生的前景增添了一份尊严，这是任何顺利的成功都不能做到的。

读书笔记

34 Suppose Someone Gave You a Pen
假如有人送你一支笔

Suppose someone gave you a pen—a sealed, solid-colored pen. You couldn't see how much ink it had. It might run dry after the first few **tentative** words or last just long enough to create a **masterpiece** (or several) that would last forever and make a difference in the scheme of things. You don't know before you begin. Under the rules of the game, you really never know. You have to take a chance!

Actually, no rule of the game states you must do anything. Instead of picking up and using the pen, you could leave it on a shelf or in a drawer where it will dry up, unused. But if you do decide to use it, what would you do with it? How would you play the game? Would you plan and plan before you ever wrote a word? Would your plans be so **extensive** that you never even got to the writing? Or would you take the pen in hand, plunge right in and just do it, **struggling** to keep up with the **twists** and turns of the **torrents** of words that take you where they take you? Would you write **cautiously** and carefully, as if the pen might run dry the next moment,

假如有人送你一支笔，一支不可拆卸的单色钢笔。看不出里面究竟有多少墨水。或许在你试探性地写上几个字后它就会干涸，或许足够用来创作一部影响深远的不朽巨著（或是几部）。而这些，在动笔前，都是无法得知的。在这个游戏规则下，你真的永远不会预知结果。你只能去碰运气！

事实上，这个游戏里没有规则指定你必须要做什么。相反，你甚至可以根本不去动用这支笔，把它扔在书架上或是抽屉里让它的墨水干涸。但是，如果你决定要用它的话，那么你会用它来做什么呢？你将怎么来进行这个游戏呢？你会不写一个字，老是计划来计划去吗？你会不会由于计划过于宏大而来不及动笔呢？或者你只是手里拿着笔，一头扎进去写，不停地写，艰难地随着文字汹涌的浪涛而随波逐流？你会小心谨慎地写字，好像这支笔在下一个时刻就可能会干涸；还是装作或相信这支笔能够永远写下去而信手写来呢？

Suppose Someone Gave You a Pen
假如有人送你一支笔

or would you pretend or believe (or pretend to believe) that the pen will write forever and proceed accordingly?

And of what would you write: Of love? Hate? Fun? **Misery**? Life? Death? Nothing? Everything? Would you write to please just yourself? Or others? Or yourself by writing for others? Would your strokes be **tremblingly** timid or **brilliantly** bold? Fancy with a **flourish** or plain? Would you even write? Once you have the pen, no rule says you have to write. Would you **sketch**? **Scribble**? **Doodle** or draw? Would you stay in or on the lines, or see no lines at all, even if they were there? Or are they?

There's a lot to think about here, isn't there?

Now, suppose someone gave you a life...

你又会用笔写下些什么呢：爱？恨？喜？悲？生？死？虚无？万物？你写作只是为了悦己？还是为了悦人？抑或是借替人书写而悦己？你的落笔会是颤抖胆怯的，还是鲜明果敢的？你的想象会是丰富的还是贫乏的？甚或你根本没有落笔？这是因为，你拿到笔以后，没有哪条规则说你必须写作。也许你要画素描？乱写一气？信笔涂鸦？画画？你会保持写在线内还是线上，还是根本看不到线，即使有线在那里？嗯，真的有线吗？

这里面有许多东西值得考虑，不是吗？

现在，假如有人给予你一支生命的笔……

单词解析 Word Analysis

tentative ['tentətɪv] *adj.* 试探性的；尝试性的

例 Political leaders have reached a tentative agreement to hold a preparatory conference next month.
政治领导人已就下个月举行预备会议达成初步协定。

masterpiece ['mɑːstəpiːs] *n.* 杰作，名作；杰出的事

例 The whole thing was a masterpiece of crowd management.
整件事情就是人群管理的典范。

extensive [ɪk'stensɪv] *adj.* 广阔的，广大的；范围广泛的

例 When built, the palace and its grounds were more extensive than the city itself.
建成时，宫殿及其庭园比城市本身面积还要大。

struggle ['strʌgl] *vi.* 奋斗；搏斗；努力；争取

例 They had to struggle against all kinds of adversity.
他们不得不同一切困境做斗争。

twist [twɪst] *vt.* 扭成一束；搓，捻；绕，卷

例 Her hands began to twist the handles of the bag she carried.
她双手开始捻弄手提包的拎带。

torrent ['tɒrənt] *n.* 奔流，急流；爆发

例 The rain came down in torrents, and we could see nothing.
大雨倾盆而下，我们看不见任何东西。

cautiously ['kɔːʃəslɪ] *adv.* 小心翼翼地；小心地，谨慎地

例 It was his custom to approach every problem cautiously.
他习惯谨慎地处理每一个问题。

misery ['mɪzəri] *n.* 痛苦；不幸

例 All that money brought nothing but sadness and misery and tragedy.
那笔钱带来的只有伤心、痛苦和悲剧。

tremblingly [t'remblɪŋlɪ] *adv.* 颤抖地，发抖地

例 Thus, it was almost tremblingly that she resumed her lover's arm.
所以当她重新挽她情人的臂膀的时候，她几乎有点发抖了。

brilliantly ['brɪlɪəntlɪ] *adv.* 灿烂地，出色地

例 In this new book, Harrison brilliantly disentangles complex debates.
在这本新作中，哈里森巧妙地理顺了那些纷繁复杂的争论。

flourish ['flʌrɪʃ] *n.* 挥舞，挥动；花样，华丽的辞藻

例 The plant flourishes particularly well in slightly harsher climes.

Suppose Someone Gave You a Pen 34
假如有人送你一支笔

这种植物在气候条件稍差一点的地区长势尤其好。

sketch [sketʃ] v. 速写；草拟；简述

例 Clare and David Astor are sketching a view of far Spanish hills.
克莱尔和戴维·阿斯特正在画远处西班牙山峦的风景素描。

scribble ['skrɪbl] n. 乱写，乱涂

例 She scribbled a note to tell Mum she'd gone out.
她匆匆写了个便条告诉妈妈她已外出。

doodle ['du:dl] vi. 心不在焉地乱写乱画

例 No, I don't think so. I no longer doodle on the wall.
不，我不这么看。我不再往墙上涂鸦了。

语法知识点 Grammar Points

① **It might run dry after the first few tentative words or last just long enough to create a masterpiece (or several) that would last forever and make a difference in the scheme of things.**

本句中 that 引导定语从句，先行词为 a masterpiece (or several)；run dry 表示 "用完了"；make a difference 表示 "有影响；起（重要）作用"。

例 Streams had run dry for the first time in memory.
记忆中，小溪第一次干涸了。

I believed that I can make a difference in this world.
我也坚信世界一定会因我而不同。

② **Instead of picking up and using the pen, you could leave it on a shelf or in a drawer where it will dry up, unused.**

本句中 instead of 后接动名词，表示 "而不是"。

例 Instead of modelling, they are copying.
他们利用复制的方法代替建模。

where 在句中做关系副词，引导定语从句。

例 England is one of the few countries where people drive on the left.
英国是少数沿左侧开车的国家之一。

③ Or would you take the pen in hand, plunge right in and just do it, struggling to keep up with the twists and turns of the torrents of words that take you where they take you?

本句中 keep up with 表示"紧跟；跟上"。

例 She was skipping to keep up with him.
她连蹦带跳地走着，好跟上他的步伐。
Penny tended to work through her lunch hour in an effort to keep up with her work
为了把活儿干完，彭妮常常午饭时间也要工作。

④ There's a lot to think about here, isn't there?

本句为反义疑问句，含be(is, are, was, were)动词的反义疑问句其句型是：
句型1：主语+ be+其他，isn't (aren't, wasn't, weren't)+ 主语？
句型2：主语+ be not+其他，is (are, was, were) + 主语？

例 There is an old picture on the wall, isn't there?
在墙上有一幅古画，是不是？

经典名句 Famous Classics

1. The road of life is like a large river, because of the power of the currents, river courses appear unexpectedly where there is no flowing water.
人生的道路就像一条大河，由于急流本身的冲击力，在从前没有水流的地方，冲刷出崭新的意料不到的河道。

2. Dare and the world always yields. If it beats you sometimes, dare it again and again and it will succumb.
你勇敢，世界就会让步。如果有时它战胜你，你要不断地勇敢再勇敢，它就会屈服。

3. Make yourself a better person and know who you are before you try and know someone else and expect them to know you.
在你想了解别人也想让别人了解你之前，先完善并了解自己。

4. Diligence is the mother of good luck; If plough deep while sluggards sleep, you will have corn to sell and to keep.

勤奋是幸运之母；如果懒汉睡觉的时候你深耕土地，你就会有谷物出售和储存。

5. If they throw stones at you, don't throw back, use them to build your own foundation instead.
   如果别人朝你扔石头，就不要扔回去了，留着做你建高楼的基石。

6. It is the same with man as with the tree. The more he seeks to rise into the height and light, the more vigorously do his roots struggle earthward, downward, into the dark, the deep — into evil.
   其实人跟树是一样的，越是向往高处的阳光，它的根就越要伸向黑暗的地底。

读书笔记

我的励志美文：梅花香自苦寒来

读书笔记